In this book, Philip Cameron writes a moving story of how he came to love the abandoned, hurting children in Romania. God led him on a miraculous journey enabling his ministry to provide safe and loving homes, education, and loving guidance for teenage girls in dangerous peril, living on the streets in Romania, Moldova, and other countries. This book is a must read and will change your life. It will refire your passion for missions and for the plight of less fortunate children in need of an earthly dad who can lead them to the Father's love.

—Marcus D. Lamb, Founder,
President Daystar Television Network

If the passion of a man is truly a reflection of the God-given heart of that man, then Philip Cameron's heart is infinite in its capacity. His heart for children continues to expand beyond reason and limits. The theme of his life has been "give me a heart for others." I have personally witnessed his passion and unlimited love for the neglected and forgotten children of this world. When I saw Philip's vision firsthand, I knew we had to help him make it happen. Thank you, Philip, for making the world a better and brighter place for thousands of children and for those of us who witness that miracle of love.

—Dr. Garth W. Coonce, President TCT Network

When you read the stories of these girls and how God has transformed them completely, you will realize that this is a miracle in our current generation. In the challenges of the world we live in today, this is an unprecedented story of the grace and mercy of God. You will laugh and you will cry, but you will never be the same!

—Bishop Paul D. Zink, Founder,
New Life Christian Fellowship and Providence School

God called my friend "with the huge heart" to Moldova to rescue children who had been thrown into the garbage heaps of humanity. Philip has been faithful to that call. You will love his story contained in this remarkable book.

—Dan Betzer, First Assembly of God,
Ft. Myers, Florida

OUR BUMMER LAMB

A Story of Love, Redemption and Rescue

PHILIP D. CAMERON

Our Bummer Lamb; a story of love, redemption and rescue.
By Philip Cameron

Scripture marked NASB is taken from the NEW AMERICAN STANDARD BIBLE®, Copyright © 1960, 1962, 1963, 1968, 1971, 1972, 1973, 1975, 1977, 1995 by The Lockman Foundation. Used by permission.

Scripture marked NIV is taken from THE HOLY BIBLE, NEW INTERNATIONAL VERSION®, NIV® Copyright © 1973, 1978, 1984, 2011 by Biblica, Inc.™ Used by permission. All rights reserved worldwide.

Scripture marked KJV is taken from the King James Version of the Bible.

Published by
The Orphan's Hands
P.O. Box 35
Clinton, TN 37717
+1 (334) 456-5544
Email: philipcameron@theorphanshands.org
Websites: www.philipdcameron.com
www.theorphanshands.org

This book or parts thereof may not be reproduced in any form, stored in a retrieval system, or transmitted in any form by any means—electronic, mechanical, photocopy, recording, or otherwise—without prior written permission of the publisher, except as provided by United States of America copyright law.

Copyright © 2020 by Philip Cameron
All rights reserved
ISBN: 978-0-578-66430-9
Printed in the United States of America

Table of Contents

Introduction 1
Chapter 1: The Babies Are Dying 4
Chapter 2: No Orphanages? 16
Chapter 3: Heart Attack! 27
Chapter 4: A Heritage of Miracles 33
Chapter 5: This Is Your Son 47
Chapter 6: Against All Odds 54
Chapter 7: The Journey for Andrew 59
Chapter 8: No Way 77
Chapter 9: The End of the Line 83
Chapter 10: The Baby with No Country 94
Chapter 11: TV Meets Orphan 104
Chapter 12: Hincesti Orphanage, Freezing Babies 117
Chapter 13: What's That Blue Sign? 122
Chapter 14: Can We Call You Mom and Dad? 133
Chapter 15: The Valley of the Shadow of Death 144
Chapter 16: A Home for Them 155
Chapter 17: Dasa's Cousin Andrei 169
Chapter 18: America 171
Chapter 19: Vatra Village 181
Chapter 20: Outreach Center 188

Chapter 21: The Bummer Lamb Reward...................194

Afterthought...198

Human Trafficking Statistics.......................................202

Appendix 205

Introduction

The tractor would trundle along the country lanes that separated the green fields that lay around the small fishing village that was home in the northeast of Scotland. It was a ritual of spring we had done for years; it was also done out of necessity. At the bends in the road, the trailer being towed would lurch, catapulting turnips into the grass. The farmer, unaware of his loss continued on. I, on the other hand, would jump into action! Mom would stop our little grey Vauxhall van and I would race to the spot where the big sweet turnip had landed. Sometimes fortune would smile and there would be two or on rare occasions three! I'd clamber back into the seat, pleased with my harvest.

Dad had been called to preach the day he'd been redeemed by grace, but preaching was a poor way to provide for your family in Scotland and the rest of the UK. In order to help out with the bills, Mom had boarders in our house. From these sporadic guests, Dad would come home, stay a while, then go again to preach the Gospel that had broken two centuries of alcoholic bondage that held the Camerons enslaved. We never felt lack. In fact, I'd feel sorry for the other boys in my class. Alan Smarts' dad owned the biggest car dealership in our town. Robert Lawries' dad the fruiteries. My dad rescued the lost from the dungeons of hell. No comparison!

Mom made games out of our lack. One time I came home to find her looking in drawers in the kitchen. When she saw me, her eyes lit up. "We need a shilling for the gas meter! Let's see if we can find S&H green stamps!" It was made to feel like fun; to her, looking back, it must have been desperate days. When the stamps were put in their place in the little booklet, stuck side by side until the two pages were full, you could hand it to the clerk at the grocery store and get the one shilling deducted from the bill. Mom was too proud to go and get the shilling, but a wee boy could do it without anyone knowing of the poverty that caused the errand. I came home, holding the shilling, and mom put it into the gas meter; we could have supper, and heat till the shilling ran out. Every few months the gas man would come, empty the meter and apply it to the bill. Turnips, found by the side of a country lane, were free.

The turnip harvest coincided with another miracle, the lambing season. Mom would stop at the gate of a field and we'd sit on top of the gate and watch lambs being born. It was miraculous. In a few minutes, a shaky little lamb would be transformed into a jumping running bundle of joy. We'd laugh at their antics. Life was amazing. Sometimes, however, things would go wrong. You'd spot it immediately. The mother didn't want her lamb. Instead of licking and nudging her baby, the ewe would walk away. When the newborn baby lamb would follow and try to feed, it would be kicked or butted. Eventually after being abused and rejected, the little lamb would stand alone, crying in the middle of the field. These lambs were known as "bummer lambs."

We'd watch, I confess sometimes with tears, knowing that unless the farmer came soon, the precious life would be lost through hunger and cold. March in Scotland can be bitter. Across the field we'd watch, and if the farmer had been watching as well, he'd come over and pick up the rejected bummer lamb and slip it into his coat. It didn't matter the mess the wee thing was in; it was now safe. The shepherd had rescued the bummer lamb! It would stay in his house with him. He would feed it warm milk, and in the evening, the shepherd would lay the lost lamb on his chest so the lamb could hear his heartbeat. Eventually the lamb would be able to return to the flock, made strong by the shepherd's care. However, from the day the lamb was returned to the flock, when he heard the shepherd come, he was always the first at the gate. Of all the sheep in the field, that bummer lamb had a closeness to the shepherd; its needs created a love for its redeemer.

So it is. We have found a world of bummer lambs in Romania, Moldova and Ukraine, rejected by those who should love them. This book is the story of love, redemption and rescue. It will touch the "bummer lamb" who lives in all of us.

PHILIP CAMERON

Chapter 1
The Babies Are Dying

IT WAS FEBRUARY, ONE of my favorite times of the year in Alabama. There was no need for air-conditioning or heat, and signs of flowers just starting to bud were everywhere. My short drive home from the office was lovely.

I pulled into the driveway, climbed out of my car, and slowly made my way to the door, taking in a deep breath of the pleasant air. Southern Alabama was nothing like the wet, raw climate of Scotland, where I was raised. I loved the feeling.

Chrissie was busy in the kitchen when I passed through the foyer, and the smell of roast beef and potatoes filled the air. After greeting her with a quick kiss on the cheek, I headed to the back bedroom, kicked off my loafers, and quickly changed my clothes. I was more than ready to settle in front of the television set in my easy chair and numb the day's happenings with The Cosby Show or Matlock as soon as the news was over.

From down the hall, I could hear the faint sound of music coming from one of the kids' rooms. A dog could be heard barking up the street. It was a normal evening in 1990 in the Cameron household. After stepping over a few of the kids' toys, I settled into my chair. As I popped up the footrest, the clock on the mantel struck 5:30, and the evening news with Peter Jennings filled the screen. Then, the phone rang.

The shrill ringing rose above all of the other commotion in the house, demanding attention like a toothache.

I stared at the receiver beside me and held my breath for a second, wanting the phone to stop ringing and my blood pressure not to rise. It wasn't the phone itself that was the problem. The problem was I knew who was calling, and I knew what he was going to say. Chrissie poked her head around the door to make sure I was by the phone and would answer it. "Yes," the look on my face said as I nodded, "I will answer. But I don't want to."

Ring! Ring!

"Hel-"

"Philip," I heard before I could finish saying hello, "babies are dying." After a short pause, "Philip, are you there?" he started again. "Did you to hear me? Babies are dying, and you have to do something!"

The voice belonged to my beloved father, Simon Cameron. Dad was one of the greatest preachers and evangelists of his day. I loved him more than life itself, but his recent calls were driving me crazy.

At sixty-six years of age, he had a recent surgery to remove cancer from his back, leaving him housebound in Scotland. Other than my mother, the only company he had was an aged Sylvania television set that was tuned to the news around the clock.

For a man who was used to being busy nonstop with ministry, the bed rest was hard to take. Half a world away, he was starting to watch the same newscast I was watching, but it was all he thought about, all he could talk about. And the lead story on every newscast was that abandoned babies were dying in Eastern Europe, especially in Romania.

The fall of Communism had come only months before. The iron curtain was finally destroyed, and detailed news from the Soviet Bloc was finally being reported to the outside world. Before the fall, no one in the Western world knew that mass orphanages filled with babies living in horrible conditions littered these countries. Suddenly, these children were featured on one television news report after the other. My dad had had a steady diet of these reports for days, and he was like a man possessed; nothing else seemed to matter to him.

"Philip, are you there?" he started again. "Did you hear me? Babies are dying, and you have to do something!"

I heard him moan in pain as he shifted in the chair. "Philip," he said before he started to weep.

From the corner of my eye, I could see Chrissie starting to set the dining room table. She'd be calling the kids, nine-year-old Philip Jr. and eight-year-old Melody, any minute. I was tired and hungry and had heard the same plea from my dad every night for a week. I kept thinking that as he began to heal, he'd start reading or writing—doing anything other than watching these blasted news reports. This obsession had to stop, or he would make both of us crazy.

"Dad, I love you, but you need to hear me. You are very, very sick. You need rest. You need to turn off the television and go to sleep. If you don't rest, you can't heal. Please. Go to bed. Let's talk tomorrow," I said as I scooted forward in my chair and started to get up. Chrissie caught my eye, and I signaled that I would be with her at the table in just a moment.

There was silence on the other end of the phone. I thought the matter was finally closed.

"Philip. Listen to me. These babies are starving to death. They are warehoused in these buildings with no one to care for them. Hundreds of them. Dying. You must do something!"

The shadow of reports out of Romania rattled in the back of my mind. A horrible man by the name of Nicolae Ceausescu, the dictator at the time, wanted to double the population of his country in a decade's time. He outlawed birth control and required every married couple to produce at least five children. The results were nightmarish.

With the explosion of birth rates in Romania, the little available food there had been was long gone. People were starving. By the thousands, babies and toddlers were left at the doors of state-run orphanages, their parents disappearing into the night.

It was tragic, no doubt about it. But it wasn't my tragedy. It was half a world away in a country I had never even visited, and rarely thought of, until my dad started this nonsense.

"This is the kind of problem governments solve—the Red Cross, the Salvation Army. The big boys handle problems like these," I tried to explain.

After listening to him ramble on for a few more moments, I'd had enough. How could I possibly help these babies from my living room in Southern

Alabama? "Dad, I have to go. Chrissie has dinner ready, and the kids are just sitting down at the table," I said. "Please, go to bed. I love you. Good night."

With both of us frustrated, I hung up and walked over to the table. Philip Jr. was already helping himself to the potatoes, while Melody was making faces at me. These were the only children I needed to worry about, had time to worry about.

I was a busy man, traveling across the country preaching the gospel in churches, on Christian television, at conferences, and at retreats. My ministry took me away from my family too much already.

God had blessed my ministry in ways that amazed me. Clearly, I was in the center of His will; how else could I explain it? People were getting saved everywhere I went. Long-lost relatives for whom I had prayed were coming back to Jesus. Scores were being healed, lives were being changed. It was all good, so very good.

Life was finally the way it was supposed to be. After years of living hand to mouth, dragging my wife and firstborn child all over the country in an RV, I enjoyed the lovely house in which we now lived. I liked driving the well-used, but well-loved, Mercedes-Benz instead of the rattletrap I'd had for years.

I had it all: ministry, family, security. Everything was good except my dad and those pesky phone calls. My mood ruined, I went to bed early in a pout and hoped the next day would be better.

Starting early the next morning, I put in a full day at my office making plans for some upcoming meetings. Over the recent years, God had anointed me to speak on the subject of household salvation, and the results had been amazing everywhere I went, making me a sought-after guest on Christian television.

As soon as I got home, tired again, but excited about my upcoming trip, the phone started ringing.

Ring! Ring!

"Philip. Babies are dying. What are you going to do about it?"

Still in my work clothes, I stood there at my wit's end. I was in no mood for this. "Look, Dad, you are sick. I am busy. Leave this alone."

Before I got the words out, he was back at me: "That's easy for you to say, my boy. If they were your babies, you would do something!"

"But, Dad, that's the point," I said, trying to calm down. "They are not my babies."

He let out a sigh. I knew that sound. I had him. I finally had him agreeing with me! Now I could eat dinner with my family without a load of guilt hanging over my head.

I was about to say good-bye when he said, "Okay, fine. Then I'll go. If you won't do something about these babies, I will. I can't turn my back on this. I can't. So if you won't go, I will." He paused for just a moment and then continued, "And if I die on the trip, it will be your fault."

He let that sink in. I tried to argue, but what more could I say? I couldn't let my dad get in a car and go to Romania any more than I could let him fly to the moon. He was too sick, too frail. He was right. The trip would kill him, but he'd do it; he would make the trip and no one or nothing would stop him. The battle was over. I had lost. I was going to Romania.

The rest of the evening was a blur. I was mad, frustrated, and looking for a target to take my frustrations out on. I barked loudly enough to clear the kids and my wife out of the living room and settled into my chair. I wanted to be alone so I could pout some more.

Leaving home was always hard for me. I loved being with my wife and family. I had everything a man could ask for. "Well, I'll do this to get my dad off my back," I told myself. "Then I can get back to real life." So I'd make the trip first to Scotland to pick up Dad, then overseas to Romania; punch the clock, as they say, and hurry back to Alabama.

The next morning, I drove to work thinking about the ramifications of the sudden trip. One pastor would be fine with rescheduling my planned visit, but the other would be upset, possibly never ask me to speak at his church again. Then there was the camp meeting to which I was supposed to fly. I had a headache just thinking about all the calls, the reactions, the impact this could have on my ministry in the future.

I pulled into the parking lot of the office at the same time as Lisa Crews, the ministry's financial manager. She would not be happy when I asked her to book my flight to Scotland and cancel all my other ones for two weeks. This last-minute trip would be costly.

Despite my worries, by noon it was all taken care of and two days later, I boarded a British Airways jet and settled in for the overnight flight. Believe me, there is no comfortable way to sleep on those planes, especially for a big guy like me. Irritated anew, I grabbed a few extra pillows and commandeered the empty seat beside me. Thank God for small favors, I thought.

I closed my eyes, and my mind immediately wandered to what was ahead of me in Scotland: my dad. I loved him so much. He was the finest man I knew. I had learned so much from him about being a man, a husband, a father, and a soul-winner. He taught by example, always being fair, Christ-centered, and kind.

Sure, I was annoyed at him about this trip, but I was worried too. As much as I hated to admit it, it would be good to see him, talk to Mom and the doctors, and see if anything more could be done to promote his healing. After the cancer had been removed, his healing had not gone as well as we'd hoped. The operation left a hole as big as a fist in his back, and it became infected, causing him much pain and suffering.

It was hard for me to wrap my head around the concept of my dad being sick. He had an amazing relationship with God. He talked to God, and God talked to him. There were times when it almost seemed like he left his body and was one with the Father.

Nibbling on the tasteless sandwich that the flight attendant placed in front of me, I decided that when

I arrived, I would show my dad the respect he deserved. No matter how silly his notion for us to go to Romania was, I would listen, be patient, and perhaps finally talk some sense into him.

The hours dragged by. I slept little on the plane. When I finally arrived in Scotland, I gathered my bags and stepped out into the cold winter air. My jacket, which had been fine in Alabama, was not quite heavy enough.

As I started toward my parents' house, I found myself anxious to see Dad. During the hour-long drive from the airport, I shook the cobwebs out of my brain as the road took me past the familiar sights of my youth. I decided I would visit with Dad and Mom, have a cup of tea and a bite to eat, and then take a nice long nap. Handling the whole "babies are dying" matter would be much easier once my batteries were recharged.

But as I pulled onto Dad's property, I was surprised to see an unusual whirlwind of activity. There were cars and trucks coming and going, all of them unloading huge boxes and bags filled with things.

"What the heck is going on here?" I asked no one in particular, looking around for someone I knew—a sibling, a cousin, someone who worked with my folks. Where was someone who could tell me what the devil was going on here? What were all of those overstuffed plastic bags? What was in those boxes? Where had all this stuff come from? And what was it for?

It didn't take long to figure it out. My dad had been quite busy from his "sickbed." Apparently, he had made calls to every pastor, every friend, and every other person he knew in Scotland about his upcoming trip. The local newspaper even carried the following headline the day before I arrived: "Cancer-Stricken Pastor to Go to Romania."

So on top of the food, clothing, and medical donations that poured in from people he knew, now total strangers were arriving with goods. The local Salvation Army gave him a truckload of diapers and supplies. The Red Cross donated baby bottles, formula, and food. Crosse & Blackwell, a giant food production company, brought five tons of canned goods. Another company gave cases and cases of oranges. People who had seen the same news stories Dad watched had come from miles and miles around. I had never seen more coats, blankets, food, and baby items in all my life.

It all seemed wonderful. Being the practical one in the bunch, I could only focus on one thing: How, for the love of God, would we get all this stuff to Romania, two thousand miles away?

Dad had small panel trucks that he used for ministry work, but nothing like what would be required to transport all of this. Only a much larger truck would hold all of these goods, but no one we knew had one of those just sitting in the driveway.

With my planned tea and nap forgotten, I went into the house for a quick visit with Dad before getting down to business. Never mind trying to talk Dad out of going; there was no fighting it now. I didn't know how, but I knew we were going to Romania.

When I walked into his room, Dad was sitting up in an overstuffed chair, leaning forward so his sore back didn't touch the cushion. With the base of the phone between his legs, he screamed into the other end of it something about packing crates.

As he finished the conversation, I tried to take in everything around me. Beside Dad's well-worn Bible, a row of pill bottles lined the nightstand. He'd lost a lot of weight since I'd seen him last, and his face was a bit ashen, his color off because of the infection. But his eyes danced with excitement. I knew that look well. Anytime my dad was moving toward a miracle, he had an unmistakable glow that no sickness could dim. I smiled in spite of myself.

Romania. Two thousand miles away. I would find out soon that in this country of twenty-two million people, there were 104,000 orphans in state-run institutions. I also would learn that what I considered a road and what Communist countries considered a road were two completely different things. I was in for a very long, hard trip, but I was blissfully unaware of these details.

After a short visit, I went down to Dad's office, pulled out a legal pad and phone book, and started the process of locating a truck. I was both shocked and pleased when the first man I called agreed at once to lease a truck to me.

It was all perfect. Too perfect.

"Just one thing," the man finished: "I need you to wire me a $100,000 deposit."

I was sure that with my overtired brain, I had misunderstood him. "Excuse me? $100,000? You must have misunderstood. I want to lease the truck, not buy it," I said.

"Mr. Cameron," the man replied, now talking to me in a tone often used with a dull-minded child, "Romania is a war zone. If my truck is going to be taken into a war zone, I must insure it."

My heart sank. This was not going to be easy. I looked out the window. More cars and trucks. More little pink blankets, cans of food, baby clothes. How the heck would I get all of this to Romania?

I hung up and started down the next listings in the phone book. Over and over, I heard the words, "Sorry, we can't help you," as soon as the word "Romania" was out of my mouth. I'd hang up, dial the next number, and repeat my then well-rehearsed speech: "Hi, my name is Philip Cameron. I assume you have been watching the news lately about the tragic situation in Romania. There are babies dying there. I am a preacher, and we have gathered food, clothing, and blankets for these babies, but we still need to find a way to get these items there. We need a truck, a big truck. Can you help me?"

No one laughed at me, but after that $100,000 bombshell, no one said yes either. I was down to one last number, for a company called Clark and Rose.

I dialed the number, delivered my spiel, and braced myself for more bad news.

"I'll get back to you in an hour," the man said.

I was so surprised, I stammered out, "You will? You'll get back to me?" After he assured me that he would call, we hung up, and I decided to go and check on my dad again. I found him on the phone, looking more tired but still yelling, a bit louder this time, into the phone. Some poor soul was being dressed down for not coming through with formula that had been promised. His determination to help these babies was amazing, and I had neither the heart nor the guts to tell him that I still had not located a truck.

Ten minutes passed, and he was still on the phone. I slowly turned and walked down the stairs, the steps creaking under my feet. I was so tired and so overwhelmed with a sense of helplessness. Feeling quite sorry for myself, I rounded the corner to the office just as the phone began to ring.

"Is this Philip Cameron?" the voice asked. "It is? Well, we have a truck for you. We at Clark and Rose want to help these babies. If you will just pay for the fuel, you can borrow the truck for as long as you need. In fact," he continued, "we will provide the drivers."

I was dumbfounded, excited, over the moon. I couldn't wait to tell Dad! What a miracle! What a breakthrough! What a God!

Chapter 2
No Orphanages?

My parents lived in Peterhead, far into the northern part of Scotland. Looking at a map of Europe, you'll notice Peterhead is about the farthest point in the United Kingdom from Romania. Finding any maps to direct us from Scotland to Romania was a challenge, as Eastern Europe had been closed to Westerners for decades.

It seemed straightforward enough, though: Go south, cross over into Belgium, and then go through Germany, east through Austria and Hungary, and finally into Romania. But we knew enough to know we had no clue what to expect.

At the end of our road trip, all we would have to go on was the name and address of a pastor in Timisoara, Romania. It was enough for my dad, so it had to be enough for me.

With the truck stuffed so full that I was sure the sidewalls were bulging, we were off. My father, brother Neil, brother-in-law John Reid, and I led the caravan in a ragtag ambulance that we'd converted into a poor man's RV, followed by professional drivers in the jampacked truck.

We started out at dawn, bags of snacks and thermoses of tea in hand. I adjusted the seat and mirrors in the van for the long trip ahead and glanced at my dad. The pain was evident on his face. Although my mom had made the bandages on his back thicker and softer to offer some comfort from the hard vinyl seat, I knew they would provide little relief.

I also knew my dad well enough to know he would not complain no matter how much agony he was in. I'd drive the "ambulance" as carefully as I could, but this trip was going to be very hard for him. After I'd agreed to make the trip, my mom, siblings, and I had all tried to talk him out of going, but there was no stopping him. He was passionate about these kids he had never met, he had worked for weeks gathering all this stuff, and he was going to see it all delivered, even if it killed him. Literally.

We turned onto the A90 a short time later. When we circled around the roundabout, I saw that my dad had fallen asleep. Silently I prayed that he'd sleep for much of the trip; it would do him good. I turned on some worship music on the portable cassette player I'd carried along and let my mind drift.

As we traveled through England, past London, and then took the ferry across the English Channel into Belgium, the roads passed through farmland and open fields, then through small villages that offered snapshots of what I pictured a bygone era to be.

Four days later, on a snowy Tuesday afternoon, we arrived in Romania. From the moment we crossed the border into Romania, we were struck by the sadness of the country. It was a country that had once been beautiful, filled with small, freshly painted houses with flower boxes on the windows and tidy lawns.

But Communism had long since broken this country. After World War II, the Soviets dealt harshly with the Romanian people. Thousands and thousands of people suspected of being enemies of Mother Russia were removed from their homes and shipped by train to the coal mines for up to ten years as "reparation" for their supposed crimes.

There were other worries for those who were left. The Communists went from one town to the next bulldozing the existing houses and replacing them with high-rise apartment-type buildings, each one as ugly and windowless as the one built before it. By design, several of these filing cabinets for humans ran off a single heating system. If there was trouble with a citizen in one building, the government would shut off the heat in all of the other buildings, making sure all the neighbors knew why. It wasn't long before the lone citizen would fall back into line.

The bulldozing process took time; every year a few thousand more houses would go down, and a few more high-rises would go up. The people who still had houses knew that it was only a matter of time before the bulldozers would be on their streets, so they stopped painting, stopped fixing the roofs.

Years went by. Children in the generation grew up watching their parents live in houses that were slowly falling apart. It became normal. All the houses that were left were crumbling, their roofs sagging and the paint chipping. No one fixed anything.

By the time Communism finally collapsed, the country had people living in two situations: either in the horrible high-rises or in broken-down houses. There was nothing else left.

As I drove across the country that dark day in 1990, the people were free of the iron fist of the Soviet Union, but they were still in bondage. The economy had collapsed along with everything else; there was no money, no banking system. The people were left with more children than they could feed, useless education, no jobs, and nothing and no one to look to for help. The government had been their only source for decades, and now it was gone.

Yes, it was a sad, sad country. While the roads along our journey had been bad, they were worse in Romania. The potholes were filled with dirty snow and ice, making it nearly impossible to see them in the light of dusk as we pulled into Timisoara. After a few U-turns and false starts, I finally found the small church we were searching for, and the pastor opened the door when we knocked.

Thankfully, he spoke enough English that we were able to communicate. "Hi, my name is Philip Cameron. This is my dad, Simon. I am hoping you can help me. We have been watching the news reports out of Romania, and we have seen the terrible condition of the orphanages. We want to help.

"In fact," I continued, pointing behind me, "we have a large truck loaded with supplies. We have food, medicine, diapers, clothes, and blankets. We just need some help. Can you direct us to the closest orphanage?"

His face was blank, completely blank. It was as though I had asked him where the nearest people with green skin lived.

Thinking perhaps he had not understood me, I repeated myself, more slowly and a little louder. I was met with the same blank stare as he shook his head.

"I don't know what you are talking about," he said. "There are no orphanages around here."

The country wasn't that large. I was stunned by what he was telling me. We were in one of the largest cities, talking to a man of the cloth, a man whose job would have been to know if the type of suffering I was talking about was anywhere near him.

"I am sorry. I have never even heard of there being orphanages around here," he continued. "Sure, there are children that are poor. We are all poor. But an orphanage with children who are dying? No."

No orphanages? The news was shocking and unwelcome. Here we were in a country we didn't know, tired to the bone with no backup plan, with Dad sicker than I wanted to believe.

In a country as desperate as post-Communist Romania, any gang of hoodlums would readily kill us to get ahold of the truckload of goods behind me. We had no names or addresses for the orphanages, and no idea where to go or what to do next. We didn't speak the language, so we had no way to get directions to a motel to sleep in that night.

"I have an idea," the pastor said as though reading my mind. "Why don't you unload the truck into the church warehouse? We have sturdy locks, and the building is well-protected. I'll direct you to a motel, you can get a good night's sleep, and tomorrow I can help you make some calls to find the best way to help children."

With great relief, I nodded my head. It would only take a few hours at best to unload the truck, and I'd finally be able to sleep. Every bone in my body ached from being in the car for so long. While the pastor went and rounded up a few locals to help us unload the truck, I found an old lumpy couch in the church for Dad to stretch out on and started making trips back and forth.

It seemed that the boxes of food and bags of clothes had multiplied during the trip. Only one other man, Ion Mehedinti, spoke any English. We started a conversation as we made trip after trip from the truck to the church warehouse. He was a tall, dark man with brown eyes and a steady smile. As we unloaded the truck, he explained some of the unique cultural beliefs that led to the country's sad shape.

"Though we lived under Communism for almost fifty years, the people clung to what Scripture they knew, or thought they knew," he explained. "One of the most damaging was the belief that women were literally saved through labor. Childbirth. They thought the more babies they had, the greater their chances of getting into heaven." This belief, coupled with the former dictator's desire to double the population, sure explained a lot.

I also learned that the layout of each of the tiny flats in the apartment-style building was identical: two rooms plus a tiny kitchen and bath. Parents typically stayed in one room, and the other room was used for as many children as they had. Everyone was crowded, hungry, and without hope that tomorrow would be any better than today. As we set down another load of boxes, Ion turned to me. "Have you ever heard of James Dobson?" It seemed like a weird question from a stranger here in the middle of nowhere. "Yes, sure I have. He is one of the best-known teachers in America. I have never met him personally, but I love his work, his heart," I responded.

"I have heard just a few of his tapes," Ion continued. "Our people need practical teaching like that on family. Communism's greatest enemy is family; they have spent generations educating the people here to depend on no one but the state, not God, not each other. I need help to teach people God's way. I'd give anything for more of James Dobson's teaching."

Reaching into his pocket, he offered me a business card. I stuffed it in my jacket pocket as he finished. "When you get back, could you see if you could send me some tapes?"

I smiled tentatively, not wanting to say no, but not wanting to commit either. The last thing I needed was another obligation. I turned to get another load and noticed later that Ion was gone; I didn't see him again that trip.

A short while later, our truck was empty, and the warehouse was full floor to ceiling. The directions to the motel were in my hand, and I couldn't wait to get there. Slowly we made our way up the road. It was dark by now, and there were no streetlights. Everything looked ominous. Still, my mood was light and improving. We had delivered the goods, and I could head home having done well by my dad.

As we pulled into the motel, I tried to hide my reaction. Had this place been in any American inner city, I would have expected to see prostitutes and drug dealers in the corner of the parking lot. I paid for the room, took the key, and got my dad inside as quickly as I could.

When I flipped on the light switch by the door, a single flickering bulb cast a dim light in the room. The floor was a worn vinyl, some color of beige or gray. It had nothing extraneous, not even a trash can. The tattered orange and green bedspreads did little to conceal the bulges and lumps in the two beds, even in the dim light.

I cleaned up as best I could in the dingy bathroom and climbed into bed, tossing a "good night" to Dad as I turned off the light.

In no real hurry to be anywhere, we slept late the next morning. I wanted Dad to get as much rest as he could before the long trip back. He moved slowly, and as he removed his nightshirt, I could see the infection leaking from his bandage. Once home, surely, he could sleep better and allow himself to rest and heal, knowing that the goods had been delivered to Romania.

After eating at a small café for breakfast, we decided to call on the pastor once more before we left. It was past noon when we returned to the church, and as we stepped out of the car, I saw the pastor running toward us from the building.

"I found it! I found it!" he shouted. With a big grin on his face, he continued, "You were right; there is an orphanage! It's right here, right down the street!"

He pointed to a gray, flat, square building less than a thousand yards from where we stood as he explained that it housed almost two hundred babies and children. This was incredible! We'd be able to hand-deliver the goods ourselves, see the joy on the children's faces. I was ready to get busy, to move the food and supplies from the warehouse to the orphanage.

As I started toward the warehouse, though, the pastor grabbed my sleeve. He couldn't quite meet my eyes. "I am sorry," he said, looking at his feet. "It's all gone."

It took a minute to sink in. Gone? "What do you mean, it's gone?" I asked. "Everything. All the food. All the clothes, coats, medicine. The people here are starving. They have nothing. I didn't know the orphanage was here, and I couldn't just sit on things that could save lives. I did what I thought I should do. I am so sorry." I didn't know whether to punch the guy or weep. Turning my back, I started to walk away, toward the orphanage. I couldn't look at him; I was afraid of what I might do or say. Instead, I focused on slowly putting one foot in front of the other. At the door, my mind flashed to all the news stories I had seen, the video of the faces, and the rows of starving children with haunting eyes. Taking a deep breath, I tried to prepare for what awaited me on the other side. In my hands, I held one lone box of formula that we'd somehow forgotten under the seat of the truck the day before—that was all I had. I had no money in my pocket beyond gas money to get home. There would be nothing on God's earth I could do for those babies that day, no matter what I found. Suddenly, I didn't want to go in. What would be the point?

I turned to my dad. "You go in if you want, but I am staying out here. I'll wait as long as you want. Take your time, and then we will go back home."

Dad looked up at me. His expression changed in an instant from that of a sick man to that of an angry, red-faced father of a rebellious child.

"You will go in there! You will go in there with me right now!" he demanded, stepping around me and swinging the door open.

As it opened, the smell of human waste assaulted me in a way I had never experienced before. It was dark inside, and I could hear metal cribs crashing into one another. The sounds of babies whimpering filled the room.

Ignoring Dad's demand, I turned my back on him and on the orphans and started back toward the truck.

"God, what on earth are You doing to me?" I muttered as much to myself as to God. "Let me go back home to my family. What am I doing here?"

I continued to walk away, calling over my shoulder, "No, Dad, I am not going in. I have nothing for them. And if I go in, if I see it and don't help, I am guilty. If I don't see it, it is someone else's problem. It's not mine."

He spun on his heels and came after me, grabbing me by the shoulders with strength I didn't know he had.

Between his teeth, he spat out, "You are already guilty. You know we have to help. You will not offend these people by not going in, and you will not disappoint the Lord and me. Now get in there."

I had no choice. My heart heavy, I walked slowly inside.

Tears started rolling down my cheek as soon as I stepped over the threshold. The smell of urine overwhelmed me. The hallway led from one massive room to the next, each filled with row after row of broken metal cribs with thin mattresses and chipped lead paint.

There were two infants in some, a single toddler in others. No child was properly clothed, especially given how cold it was. Some wore shirts; others wore nothing but tiny handkerchief-like cloths on their behinds. Their arms and legs looked like sticks, and their eyes were sunken deep into their faces.

They were covered in filth, human feces, urine, food they had thrown up. Each face was sadder than the last, surreal, beyond describing with mere words.

A few slept in spite of the horror and smell. A few stared off into nothingness, not making a sound, not moving a muscle, not noticing that I was there. Some of the toddlers stood holding onto the sides of their cribs, rocking with all their might. The rhythm of the crib rocking back and forth was all they had to soothe themselves.

There was not an adult to be seen in the room. These babies were alone in their misery, caged in their cribs, suffering from hunger and God knows what else.

And I had nothing to give them.

Chapter 3
Heart Attack!

We didn't leave that day. Instead, we spent a few painful hours at the orphanage before heading back to the motel again, planning to go to bed early and start our trip home as rested as possible.

The next morning, Dad looked worse. He said little, his skin was ashen, and the spark in his eyes had gone. But that didn't stop me from barking at him to hurry along.

"I am leaving here in thirty minutes," I said as soon as my feet hit the floor. I'd gotten little sleep, and my emotions were riding a roller coaster of anger and sadness, helplessness, and—dare I admit it— shame. "If you aren't in the van by then, I am leaving without you," I blurted out.

A few minutes later, Dad limped through the chill morning air toward the van. It was starting to snow, and as soon as he climbed in, he closed his eyes. I was glad to see him nap—I was in no mood to chat. My whole world had been rattled from what I had seen and experienced at that orphanage.

So much had come at me so fast that I hadn't had time to digest it. As we started up the road, my mind wandered back in spite of my best efforts to think of anything else.

Were those really coffee cans that were being used to potty train the little ones? A row of cans lined the walls, the metal edges jagged, the tops cut off with some sort of crude can opener. Over time, the metal rusted, and the labels faded.

I had watched a lone worker take all of the children who were old enough to stand and force them to sit their naked little bums on these cans. She lined up twenty or more, and under her iron rule, the children would sit on those cans for hours at a time.

My heart stopped each time a child rebelled for a moment and stood up. Deep cuts, the same shape and size as the tops of the cans, were swollen, raw, and oozing with infection across their tiny bottoms. Worse still, the monster of a woman in charge couldn't have cared less. She'd take them by the arms and violently force them back down on the cans, ignoring their pleas, their pain. How could she be so heartless?

Behind me, Dad let out a moan and shifted in his sleep. My thoughts turned to him. How was he handling what he saw? I'd never even given him a chance to really talk. As sick as he was, I knew his heart was aching for those babies more now than before he'd seen them himself. All that work, all the calls, the favors, and for what? We hadn't helped the babies at all. I had wasted two weeks of my life, and no telling how much in airfare and lost income, and for what? To have the stuff taken from us without a bit of resistance. Disgusting, all of it.

Hours passed, and Dad still slept. Should I be worried? He'd slept all night, and now most of the day, but maybe sleep was what he needed. The cassette player was off, so it wouldn't disturb him, leaving nothing to invade my thoughts but what I had seen and smelled in Romania.

With no soap, the only way the workers could "clean" the make-shift diapers was by rinsing them out in cold water and hanging them over the luke-warm radiators to dry. To minimize the number of diaper changes, the workers gave the babies as little water or formula as they could get away with. The few drops each child received several times a day was just enough to keep them alive, but never enough to satisfy them.

Not only were the children malnourished and dehydrated, but they were also in constant pain, too weak to cry on death's doorstep. Who cares?

"Really, who cares that these children are dying?" I said. My words, which I'd meant to keep to myself, caused Dad's eyes to flutter open.

"My Jesus cares," he said, and drifted back to sleep. I felt my eyes get hot with a flush of tears.

Two days, several shifts of drivers, and roadside stops blended together. We made good time, and as light was starting to break on the third morning, the signs announced that London was less than an hour away. Thankfully, we'd have time to get a real breakfast and still get to the other side of the city before heavy workday traffic slowed us down. I noticed a truck stop and waved over the eighteen-wheeler behind me. With any luck, it would be the last stop of the trip. Inside, tables of steaming eggs, toast, sausages, and bacon lined up before us. It was the first real meal we'd had since leaving Scotland.

Dad and the others settled into a back booth with their trays as I made my final selections. Just as I turned to follow them, I felt a stirring within me. I don't say this lightly, but the voice of the Lord spoke to me.

"Don't sit there with your dad. Sit on the other side, alone. Over there," I felt Him saying. Following His leading, I set my tray down, then went back to let my dad know I would not be joining him. I told him I was fine, not upset; I just needed a moment or two alone.

Across from where I had left my tray was a table of men, and I turned my back to ignore them. Just as I lifted my warm cup of tea to my lips, I heard one of them utter the name of the Lord. With my emotions and nerves already on edge, I responded instantly, my head snapping around to face them. How dare someone use the name of my Lord and Savior in vain? I was going to give them a piece of my mind! But as I started to stand, I heard him complete his thought: "Preach the gospel . . ."

Now I was curious. We weren't exactly in a Communist country anymore, but someone speaking of the Lord in a public area like this was not something you heard often in the United Kingdom. I went over and introduced myself to the three men.

"Hi, my name is Philip Cameron," I said. "I am a preacher from Scotland, but I live in the United States now. I couldn't help but overhear you talk about the Lord."

They each shook my hand and smiled. As they introduced themselves, I learned that one was a top executive for James Dobson. James Dobson! It seemed surreal. I patted my jacket and found the business card from Ion still there.

"It's a long story," I explained, "but I am on my way back from Romania. The people there are hungry for teaching, especially about family, which is Dr. Dobson's specialty."

Handing him the card, I went on, "This man is a lay leader in his church, and he asked me specifically if I could send him some James Dobson teaching material when I got home. Could you help him?" He agreed to do what he could for a man who was a complete stranger to us both.

I finished my breakfast with a lighter heart. I had heard from God. He spoke to me, I listened, and a Christian brother in Romania would have his prayers answered.

It felt good—especially because I was not exactly proud of how I had responded to His call over the last few weeks. I had not treated my dad with the honor and respect he deserved. I had not responded with joy at the thought of making a difference on this trip, and I was still mad at God because all of our gifts had been taken. We had enough to change the lives of those babies. Why did God allow us to get so much and come so far just to have this happen? I didn't get it. I was angry, but I was relieved to know God still spoke to me . . . and I could hear Him! Twelve hours later, we arrived home. Mother greeted us before I could even get Dad's door open. Every bone in my body ached, screaming for a good night's sleep. I forgot to be polite, to help, to even unload my personal items from the car. I walked straight into the house and up the stairs and fell on the bed in my room. That is the last thing I remembered for twelve hours.

When I finally awoke, it was 6:00 in the morning. Outside the birds were chirping, but oddly that was the only sound I could hear. By this time, I would typically smell breakfast cooking or hear the teapot whistling. Had Mom overslept? I noticed that she had washed the clothes I'd been wearing the night before and had hung them on the back of the door. I wasn't worried, but I did think it was strange.

I took a shower and dressed in the clothes Mom washed. Taking my time, I made the bed and tossed the dirty clothes into my suitcase, thinking only about the flight schedules and what I needed to do before I could finally fly home.

"Mom?" I called as I walked down the steps. "Mom, are you there?" Silence.

Knowing she'd be awake, I knocked on her bedroom door. She had had her quiet time at five o'clock every morning of my life.

"Mom?" Still no answer.

I opened the door to an empty room.

Across the hall, the bathroom door was open, but she wasn't in there either. In the kitchen, there was no sign of life. Where the heck was Mom? And where was Dad, for that matter? It was too early for them to be out and about, and it was totally unlike Mom not to have things started for breakfast by now. A tiny dart of fear flew across my heart. Something was wrong, I could feel it. But what?

Walking out the door, I found my brother-in-law John, getting out of his car. "Where are Mom and Dad?" I asked before even saying hello.

"Philip, hi. I am sorry; don't you know? Your dad had a major heart attack. They tried to wake you, but they couldn't get a rise out of you. They couldn't wait any longer, so they rushed him to the hospital hours ago."

Chapter 4
A Heritage of Miracles

Heart attack?

This just didn't make sense. Closing my eyes for a split second, I tried to process what I'd just heard.

I should have known this was coming. After all, we had been side by side for almost ten days, night and day! Sure, I knew that he was uncomfortable, but he was recovering from cancer surgery; of course he was uncomfortable. If he'd ever asked me to stop, to find a doctor or hospital, I would have.

Back inside, the house was eerily quiet without Mom and Dad. Suddenly, I felt like a little boy, abandoned, all alone. My dad was my rock; there was no one on earth I respected more. He was a part of me that went beyond father and son. Every sermon I had ever preached, every praise song I had ever written or sung, was because this man poured his life, his love of Jesus, his ministry, into me.

"Dear Lord," I prayed, "please don't let him die. It's too soon. I need him. My kids need him. This world needs him."

Knowing him as well as I did, it was hard to fathom that my father was not born into a household of believers. For the past two hundred years, probably every male in his family had been a worthless alcoholic. The stories about those bad boys were legendary. The Camerons were the town drunks. Everyone knew they would be first in line at the bar. If there was a fight, they started it. If there was someone in the gutter at the end of the night, it was a Cameron.

The name Cameron meant "worthless" in my hometown for generations. Dad's generation didn't start out any better. Dad's older brother, Michael, was a good-looking chap, shorter than Dad and stouter. He was a decade older than my father, and by the age of eighteen he was a full-blown alcoholic.

My grandfather served in the military, and Michael was hired by the military as he came of age. His time in the service gave him nothing but money and freedom to develop his alcoholism further. Every weekend that he was on leave, he would travel by ferry to the mainland and head to a smoky bar. He was no "life of the party" drunk.

No, he would buy a bottle of rum, find a quiet place to sit in the corner, and drink until he passed out. When he came to, he'd drink some more until he passed out again. That was his life. As the weekend neared its end, he would somehow manage to drag himself back on a bus, nod off during the trip back to base, and muddle through the week until he could do it all again.

Even in his youth, the effects that the alcohol had on him were beginning to show. He felt terrible. His weight dropped, his skin looked yellow, and he had no will to live. His life revolved around the bottle, and there was no room for anyone or anything else.

But during one of these trips, something happened. One Monday morning, as he was waiting to catch a bus to a party, Michael realized he was hungry and had a little time. After walking into a quaint little tea shop, he settled at one of the tables by the window. After a quick look at the menu, he ordered a cup of tea and a sandwich.

While waiting for the waitress to return with his tea, something caught his eye. There, settled between the salt and pepper shakers, was a folded pamphlet. Mindlessly, he picked it up and began to read, "For God so loved the world, that He gave His only begotten Son" (John 3:16, NASB).

In that instant, the Holy Spirit convicted him, and he began to weep and shake as he read the Scriptures for the very first time. Tears began to slide down his cheeks and onto the lace tablecloth. The waitress approached with his tea and immediately saw the tears.

Sinking into the chair beside him, the older lady looked into his eyes, took his hand, and asked, "Son, are you saved?"

He didn't know how to explain it, but he knew the Holy Spirit was working in him. He looked up and said, "Yes, I am; I'm saved!"

By the power of God, he was delivered instantly. He was released from the chains the demon of alcoholism had him in for so long.

The bus came and went, but he stayed to talk to the woman. "Where are these words from?" he asked, pointing to the pamphlet.

"They're from the Bible, son." The woman's kindness was evident in her words.

With John 3:16 fresh in his mind, my Uncle Michael met Jesus in that tea shop. The Cameron family has never been the same.

When he returned to the island, he began knocking on every door during his off hours, saying, "I've met a man called Jesus, and He saved me. I found the words in this book, the Bible. Will you read it? You might find Him too."

The very next weekend, he went to visit his family with a beat-up red suitcase full of Bibles and a heart desperate to introduce his family to his Savior.

"We don't have to live like this," he announced to a less-than-enthusiastic gathering of his parents, aunts, uncles, and siblings—including my dad. Many of them stared at him from a haze of some stout drink.

"Really," he implored, "we don't have to be drunks!"

It wasn't a pleasant weekend for any of them, and he left feeling like he had made no progress and his family members were just happy to have him off their backs.

He returned to Stroma at the end of his leave, disappointed by his family's reaction, but determined, nonetheless. For seven years, he tried to reach his family for Jesus. For seven years, his whole family tried to talk him out of being a "religious fanatic."

But nothing stopped Michael. His prayers, along with my mother's devotion years later, eventually led to Dad's belief in Christ. From the time he was saved, Dad had spent his entire adult life helping others, preaching, and sharing what God had done for him. He was a powerful force in the pulpit, a natural speaker, despite never being formally trained, and mentored more young preachers than anyone else I have ever met.

The thought of him on an operating table with his chest split open flashed in my mind. This just couldn't be happening to Dad!

Again, I prayed, pleading with God to save his life. I was scared and hopping mad. How dare they not wake me when this happened? My dad had a heart attack, and they took him out of the house without even bothering to wake me! I could feel my blood beginning to boil. The conversation would not be pretty when I got to the hospital.

I had no idea if they had taken Mom's or Dad's car—or maybe even someone else's—and I didn't know where to start looking for a set of keys. Maybe on his dresser? No. Hanging by the kitchen door? No. I finally found a set in a candy dish on a hallway table.

Both car keys were on the ring, side by side. It figured. My parents were just like that. They really were a storybook couple.

I'd known from the time I was a little boy that I wanted a marriage like theirs. I wanted someone to look at me like that, someone who still made my heart flip decades after we wed. I wanted a best friend, someone who understood God's leading in my life and helped me follow those leadings. I found all that and more in my Chrissie. But without them as a model, I would never have known what to look for. I'd heard their story a hundred times. They'd met at Uncle Michael's wedding in 1947. Mother had dressed with great care that night, as she always did.

Her flame red hair was curled perfectly, and she wore a simple string of pearls to complement her light blue dress and black heels.

The band was playing a Perry Como tune that was just right for dancing, and my mom and her date were swaying to the music in the middle of the dance floor. As they danced, she put her head on his shoulder and scanned the room, mindlessly looking to see if any of her other friends had arrived.

It was then that she first saw my father, standing among others with his back against the wall. He was tall and thin, with thick wavy hair—a good-looking kid who stood out in any crowd.

She tapped her date on the shoulder and pointed toward them. "Who is that? I don't think I've ever seen them before," she asked innocently enough.

"Harrumph," her date snorted. "They are Camerons. They're not good people, no one you'd want to talk to. Hard to believe my cousin just married into that bunch." With that, he grabbed her waist a bit tighter and turned her away from them as the two of them danced.

His words and actions unnerved her. During the song, she stopped dead in her tracks in the middle of the dance floor. "Excuse me, but who do you think you are, telling me whom I should or should not talk to? I am not a child, and I do not belong to you!" she sputtered, her eyes flashing with rage.

To make her point, she made her way across the floor and soon was dancing with my Uncle John, and later with Dad. The music played on. Frank Sinatra. Nat King Cole. Romance was in the air. Before the night was over, she was quite taken with my father, and he with her.

For months they dated, fell in love, and were practically inseparable. Dad was just sixteen, and my mom was eighteen. Then, two unthinkable things happened: Dad received an official government mailing that announced he had been conscripted into the army, and at the same time, my mother began to suspect that she was pregnant.

My father recalled my mother walking into Dr. Dingwall's office—the town family doctor—dressed as if she were about to be photographed for a fashion magazine, with her hair just so, wearing red high heels and a stunning formfitting dress.

Dad walked her to the front door and stayed outside to wait. To my father, the minutes seemed like hours as he stood watching, waiting. Then the front door opened. Mother stood straight and tall, trying to appear confident as she walked out the door. He was at her side in a few strides, and she wasted no time telling him the news.

"I am pregnant."

They walked in silence back to her house. When they arrived, she didn't even slow down, stepping inside and closing the door before Dad could say a word, much less follow her.

Helplessly feeling like his world had just exploded, my dad walked home. Scared and clueless about what to do next, he walked into his house and explained to his mother what had happened.

"I am going to marry her," he announced. "She is having my baby, and we need to get married right away."

"You will do no such thing, young man," his mother replied, turning on her heel and slamming the door behind her.

As my father told the story years later, he knew from the look on her face that this would not be discussed any longer. His mother was stern and set in her ways. She controlled the family with an iron fist. Dad knew there was no fighting her. He could not win, nor could he live without my mom. Heartbroken, he began to weep. He thought of the love of his life alone with a baby, his child, growing inside her, and the tears turned to wails of grief.

Heartbroken and desperate, my father locked himself in the tiny bathroom. He wanted to die, for the pain to stop. He grabbed a bottle of pills and swallowed a fistful of aspirin. When his parents finally got the bathroom door open, he was vomiting all over the floor.

As the waves of nausea settled down hours later, he looked up from his seat on the bathroom floor to a sight he had never seen in his sixteen years: his mother crying.

His father put his arms around him and rocked him back and forth like he was cradling a child. "Don't do this, son," he pleaded. "We love you. You are a man now, and if you love this girl, of course you can marry her."

Seven months later, in 1948, the young married couple was living behind my grandparents' house in a tiny six-by-twelve-foot room with no running water and a single cord that brought electricity from the main house, awaiting both the birth of their baby and the date that my dad would have to report for military duty.

The child, whom my parents named Simon after his father (a Scottish tradition), was a lovely boy with a tuft of reddish hair, bright blue eyes, and a round, red face. He cried loudly, ate heavily, and slept in two-hour shifts. Three days after his birth, the tiny baby stopped breathing. Immediately my mother leaped to her feet and wailed, "Simon, quick, something is wrong with the baby!"

After taking a quick look at the baby's still face, my father ran out the door and down the street. Stealing a bike along the way, he rushed to the nearest doctor's office and burst through the doors without knocking.

"Get out!" the doctor barked.

"You don't understand. My baby is dying," my dad begged.

"If your baby is dying, he will be dead before I get there," the doctor snapped coldly, turning his back on my father. "Now get out!"

Dad closed the door behind him and began weeping loudly and uncontrollably, still standing on the front step, longing to hear the doctor open the door and offer to save his baby. Sorrow turned to anger. Anger to despair. Finally, all he could do was go home and accept that his baby was gone.

Adding to the heartache, just days later on a misty gray morning, my mother watched my father board a train to boot camp. They said nothing as they stood on the platform until the final call. Each carried a pain too great to even speak. She kissed him good-bye and walked the long way back to their broken-down shack—a place that felt as empty as her heart.

While my father was away in the service, my mother busied herself with work. Among her many jobs, she took a job as a maid. During that time, two men came to town to hold a revival meeting. Their names were Donald Walker and Herbert Harrison, and they slept in a converted meat truck, making their beds on the cold metal that had once held slabs of meat. Each night, they held a revival meeting, which started a buzz across town. The Holy Spirit was moving.

Out of sheer curiosity, my mother attended a few of their services. By the time they left town, which was seven years after Michael started praying, ninety-six people had been saved. Sixty-seven of them were Camerons, including my mom.

My mother found her way to the altar when she heard the words of Matthew 16:26 (NIV): "What good will it be for someone to gain the whole world, yet forfeit their soul? Or what can anyone give in exchange for their soul?"

Jesus provided a safe harbor for this brokenhearted young woman who lost her first child and was separated from her husband so early in their marriage. Church became her whole life while my dad was serving in Trieste, Italy. Working through her grief and loneliness, she dug into the Word of

God and attended every service and Bible study she could.

Although Dad sent his paycheck home every week, my mother struggled to get by. The army paid him a single man's wages because there was no pay scale for a married man his age.

My mother and father wrote to each other often while he was deployed. Mom's letters were devoted to sharing her new faith; Dad's letters were sent with harsh commands to "get out of that religion." But my mother would counter his demands, saying she could not become "unborn."

By the time he came home in September 1951, both of my parents were very different people—strangers living under the same roof. Mom had grown closer to God each day and faithfully tithed from Dad's tiny paycheck, while my father had become an angry drunk with an eye for women. He'd order her to go with him to bars and drinking parties, and he beat her terribly if she refused. My mother was too afraid to tithe or to even attend church, fearing what he might do if he found out she was "spending money on the church."

One Saturday afternoon, she went into town with my father to pick up a few things. While he wandered off in one direction, my mother ran into some ladies from the church. They chatted a bit, catching up, and she tried to evade their questions about her attendance at church. Just as Dad came up behind her, she blurted: "I feel so guilty. I have not paid my tithes since Simon got home. We are still living in a shack behind my uncle's house. I cook on a camp stove. We sleep in a twin bed. We only have two plates, two bowls, two cups, two forks, and a few clothes. And we have a baby on the way! He would never understand."

"Understand what?" he barked from behind her. "What is a tithe, anyway?"

Mother, bracing for the outburst that was sure to follow, explained to him that the Bible teaches that we are to give ten percent of our earnings to the Lord each week,.

"So you're supposed to give God ten percent, and you have been giving nothing? You go back there and start giving fifteen percent until you make up every last penny. I can't afford to have God mad at me!" he blurted. "I am already in trouble with Him." He turned and headed back toward the house, Mother following a few steps behind.

With that, my mother started tithing fifteen percent until she was "caught up." She knew God was working on Dad. From that point on, every now and then, he would go to church with her. The preachers knew exactly the kind of life he was living and would turn up the flames of hell with their words as they preached. Dad simply sneered back at them.

Mother endured a lot in the seven years before Dad was saved. Many good Christian women would have walked out. Instead, she stayed and prayed. In 1952, she gave him a daughter, Wendy, and then she gave him me three years later.

I didn't come into the world easily. When Mom's contractions began, I was breech, racking her thin body with pain. Dr. Dingwall came to the house and stayed for days, fearful of losing us both. With nothing to ease her pain, he had to reach inside my mother and turn me around. All this was done in that tiny, crude shack in which they lived. For forty-eight hours, this kind doctor stayed with my mother, sang to her, and comforted her, until he felt we were stable enough to be on our own.

Mother was so grateful for his care. Months later, when I w.as still an infant, she started helping the doctor and his wife in their home—the same house she had often admired as a child.

Both Dr. Dingwall and his wife struggled with alcohol abuse, but it didn't deter my mother. She would help them out of bed, toss out the empty bottles of booze, prepare his office so that he could attend to patients, and get their kids ready for school.

Out of appreciation for what he had done for her, she also cleaned, cooked, and ran errands—anything she could do to serve him. My mother would care for the doctor and his wife in the mornings, and my father would spend the evenings drinking. My sister, Wendy, often would hear my mother crying while he was out.

"Lord, keep him safe tonight," Mother would pray through her tears. She continued to pray, saying, "Give me grace, God. Give me the grace to live with him one more year, one more day, one more hour."

She never knew what would set him off.

One afternoon, he stomped into their shack for his lunch, and my mother knew she was in trouble before he even opened his mouth.

"I hate you, and I hate God," he roared. "I am finished with you!" With that, he stormed out and went back to his work cutting wood.

That afternoon, the 27-inch electric saw screamed as he cut one piece of wood after the other, sawdust flying everywhere. He paused a moment to wipe his brow and check his watch. It was almost 2:00 p.m.

As he picked up another piece of wood to feed into the saw, the Holy Spirit began speaking to his heart. He'd never encountered or experienced anything like it. He began to sob. Shaking and weeping, he continued to try to feed wood into the saw, his voice rising over the noise so loudly that his brother John rushed over to see what was wrong.

"Simon, Simon, what's 'e matter with you, boy? Are you hurt? What is wrong?"

Shaking his head, all my dad could say in his Scottish dialect was, "I dinna ken." (I don't know)

"Well, get off that saw before you cut your arm off!" John said as he led him away to the shop office. After helping him onto the battered old sofa, John got him some tea and ordered him to stay there while he fetched his mother, who was close by.

In mere minutes she was there, trying to determine what was wrong with her son.

"Tell me what happened," she said.

John shook his head and told her how Simon had just started sobbing, right out of the blue. "And he kept saying the strangest thing: 'I'm not worthy. I'm not worthy,'" he explained, a bewildered look on his face. They decided to take him home to my mother, Wendy. She then asked him: "What's wrong with you, Simon?" Then it dawned on her.

Mother walked over to the sofa and put her small hand on my father's tear-stained face. "I know what is wrong with you, Simon Cameron. The Holy Ghost has got a hold on you." He looked at her, his eyes pleading for an answer. "The Bible says that if you call on the name of the Lord, you will be saved," she continued.

Dad's cry instantly transformed from a sob to a shout, "Jesus, tak' me!" (Take me) And with that, he was born again. My father was twenty-five and had been married for nine years, and suddenly, he had a new life.

I don't remember anything of my dad's past life. I was only two years old when he was saved; I have never smelled alcohol on his breath, never heard the Lord's name taken in vain, never seen him act like anything but what he was: a married Christian man who loved God and lived his life for Him.

He was a legacy. He really was. Now he was in some dreary hospital, clinging to life. And I had to get there. Fast.

Chapter 5
This Is Your Son

When I arrived at the hospital, Dad was sleeping in a bed at the far end of the ICU.

The stark white sheets made him look paler, thinner, and frailer than I had ever seen him. My heart caught in my throat as I looked at him, guilt washing over me like a wave. I wanted to cry, to scream. I wanted him to forgive me for taking so long to get to Scotland, for allowing him to go to Romania on that giant goose chase, for sleeping through his heart attack. Instead, I stood silently by his bed and prayed.

Tubes and wires attached him to the various machines behind him that bleeped as they danced to their own tune. Nurses hurried by without a word. A few beds down someone called a Code Blue, and suddenly, the room was filled with all manner of medical professionals frantically working on the patient. In spite of their efforts, the woman died.

Her passing touched me deeply, underscoring how fragile life is, especially in the ICU. How could my dad, Simon Cameron, be lying in a hospital bed so close to death?

I closed my eyes and prayed, "Dear Jesus, please heal my dad. Touch him as only You can. I love him so much, Father. I need him. We all need him. Heal him."

A noise from his bed startled me. Dad was waking up, and the tube down his throat was bothering him. He gurgled what seemed to be a few words. I moved closer and asked him to repeat himself.

A pitiful little cough escaped him, and then he repeated what he had said: "There are babies dying."

It was a moment of complete clarity. I suddenly knew exactly what I needed to do, what the Lord was saying to me, what would allow Dad to settle back, relax, and recover.

With my hand on his shoulder, I said, "Dad, I know there are babies dying. I saw them too. They are mine now. As soon as you are a little bit better, I promise I will get on a plane, go back to America, and raise the money we need to really make a difference for those orphans. They need more than a truck of food and diapers. It's going to take a lot of money, but I have lots of friends in ministries and churches, and I am going to get every last one of them involved. We'll help those babies."

Before I could get all of the words out, he was asleep again. I had no idea how much he'd heard, but it didn't matter. I made a vow to him, to the Lord, and to those Romanian babies. They were mine now.

I pulled up a chair and watched him sleep for a while, praying, thinking, planning my next moves. Suddenly, nothing on my calendar seemed appealing or exciting.

I didn't want to go on Christian television and sing happy praise songs. I didn't want to preach the salvation message to an audience surrounded by other preachers, churches, and programs that detailed the

Roman Road to Salvation every twenty minutes. Americans literally had the gospel at their fingertips; just one click of the remote, and another preacher on television would deliver the message.

All I could think about was those babies. I felt like a man who knew there was a building on fire with children inside. I had to hurry. Mind you, I had no idea how to do that, what it would cost, what governmental red tape might be involved, how I would overcome the language barrier. But my course was set. Every lost moment meant more lost lives. I had to rescue as many babies as the Lord allowed.

Two weeks later, Dad was doing better, and I was in America. I slept little, working around the clock calling every person I had ever met and asking for help for the children of Romania. I flew all over the country, zigzagging from the East Coast to the West, telling the story of what I had seen in any church that would have me. I had no photos, no videos, no handouts of what I had seen; all I had was my firsthand story, my passion, and the anointing of God.

But that was enough. The money came from all over, and I was back on that twenty-two-hour truck ride from Scotland to Romania with enough money and supplies to begin changing the lives of the babies I'd met.

Six weeks later I was back. I stood in the vestibule of the cold damp building. We started at the orphanage we found on our first trip, supplying it with food, diapers, potty-chairs, and more. We replaced the old wooden window frames so that the place would be warm through the harsh winter months. I worked with local contractors, supervising the jobs to make sure every dollar was spent properly, and watched as lives were being changed.

I was pouring cash into buildings that were owned by a Communist country, but I would not let that deter me. That wasn't the point. The point was that babies were dying of starvation and neglect.

Once the projects were well under way, we brought Christmas boxes and candies. The children's faces changed as their health improved. We were met with bright smiles and giggles on every trip back to Romania. We were delighted to see the children gaining weight, to see the color returning to their skin.

Seeing radical improvement at the first home, we set out to find another orphanage before returning to the United States.

It had snowed all night, and the day was gray and bitterly cold. The wind blew the snow across the potholed road as we navigated slowly toward a home. We had been told that it was "really bad," but after what we had already seen, how bad could it be?

The snow was falling hard, and the large, fluffy flakes made it difficult to see. When we finally arrived, I tried to open the door of the truck. It was frozen shut. I slammed my shoulder into the metal door with all my might, and with a creak it finally opened. My loafers were soaked the instant I stepped out into the snow. For a moment, I wished that for once in my life I'd worn boots.

Carefully, I stepped through the angry blizzard. I opened the gate and let myself into the yard. I had started toward the building but then stopped dead in my tracks. What was I seeing? Through the snow, I could see something—someone—outside in the yard.

"No," I told myself, "there can't be anyone sitting out in this storm, but . . ."

It was a girl, no more than five years old, sitting there all alone. As I drew closer, she looked in my direction without focus, and I could immediately tell that she had Down syndrome.

"Hi, sweetheart," I said softly as I walked toward her.

Someone—some monster—had left her tied to the old rusty chair in which she was sitting. Back and forth she rocked herself, mumbling words I could not understand. She was wearing only a thin jacket, and despite the bitter cold, she had nothing on her feet but socks with holes in them. It took a few minutes to untie her. When I was finally able to release her, she clung to me like a drowning person to a life raft.

I took her inside and found worse conditions than I had ever seen—these were babies on whom the people of Romania had given up. Many of the children were physically disabled, while others had mental disabilities. As I walked the halls, I found still others who were critically ill and dying.

No one cared. This was a warehouse for these babies; that's all it was. If there had ever been any doubt in my mind that this would be the driving passion of my life, it was settled in that moment. I'd be back again . . . and again.

My second trip was a whirlwind of hiring contractors, delivering goods, and getting to know each of the children. It was a long and slow process, but finally, I felt at peace, knowing that the children I had come to love finally would have a warm home.

Dad was healthy enough to travel with me on my third trip to Romania. I couldn't wait for him to see all that we had accomplished since our initial trip. He would hardly recognize the first place, or the children he'd met; I couldn't wait to show him.

We spent a happy afternoon delivering more goods, playing with the children, enjoying the happy sounds they made. Gone was the nasty smell that had hung in the air on our first visit. Gone was the look of hopelessness on the children's faces. Even the workers seemed happier and more engaged. They had food to feed their charges, diapers, and laundry detergent—the simple things that make all the difference.

I also showed Dad the other homes we were helping, stopping in each one long enough to visit all the children.

We walked into one upstairs room, and there, three rows back, was a little boy sucking in his cheeks. As the other children rocked back and forth in their cribs, he stood still, watching me. Locking eyes with him, I started walking toward his crib, talking to him in a singsong voice. As I neared the crib, I heard a voice as clear as a bell: "This is your son."

I was dumbstruck. I knew as well as I knew my name that I had just heard the voice of the Lord. Like Moses before the burning bush, I knew God was there; He had spoken. My life was changing.

To ground myself, I needed to let Dad know what had happened. "Dad," I said, reaching for his elbow, "Dad, look at that boy. Look at that face." Stopping, he turned with me.

Piercing green eyes stared back at us.

"Aye," said Dad as he nodded and turned his attention to a child in another bed. "He is a bonny boy."

Forcefully, I said, "No, Dad." The tone of my voice caught his attention more than the words I said. He looked at me carefully.

My voice softened, and I swallowed hard, "God wants me to adopt this boy."

I walked over and reached for the child, who looked to be no more than two years old. He was thin as a rail, and though his eyes were alert, he could barely speak a word of Romanian, and certainly could not speak English. I was astonished to learn later that he was four years old.

He practically leaped into my arms. It didn't matter that he had nothing on but a tattered old shirt or that his hair was matted to his head. It was evident the boy had not been washed in weeks; the smell was overwhelming. None of it mattered. I held him and rocked him, knowing that this was my son.

My son. God was giving me this boy.

I held him close, soothing him, falling in love with him.

Softly I spoke into his ear, "I don't know who you are or how you got here, but I promise, I will make you my son."

Chapter 6
Against All Odds

The trip home was a blur—there's not much about it that I can remember. What I do remember is being so emotionally bonded to this child that I felt physically attached to him. I knew God intended for him to be mine. Every step I took away from him, every minute on an airplane, every mile I drove toward home, took me farther away from my boy, and it was physically painful.

When I pulled into the driveway of my lovely home, I sat in the car for a moment. Just the sight of the house was usually enough to lift my spirits, especially after a long trip. That home held everything I loved most.

Everything . . . until now.

I was attached to that little boy in Romania, as if an invisible umbilical cord led from the darkest heart of that country to mine as I sat outside my sunny home.

I didn't want my family to see my face and know that I was a mess inside. Trying to gather my nerve, I opened the car door. I was aware with every breath that my announcement would change the lives in our family forever. Bringing home this baby I had fallen in love with would demand a sacrifice. No one would feel it more than my wife, but my children also would be affected.

After a few moments, I slid out of the car. Stretching my legs, I looked around the yard. Two bicycles, bright and shiny, leaned against the garage. A soccer ball, still so new that there were no scuff marks on it, rested in the high grass by the fence, and the bright yellow slide on the swing set sat invitingly in the backyard.

His name was Andrew. He was miles away in a rusty crib, rocking back and forth, back and forth, with no one, nothing. The contrast was staggering.

Blinking back a tear, I lifted my suitcase out of the car and walked quickly to the door. Chrissie was standing with her back to me at the kitchen sink, washing the supper dishes, when I arrived. Hearing me come in, she turned and smiled at me over her shoulder. Without a word, I dropped my suitcase at the door and wrapped my arms around her waist, drinking in the magic of holding her in my arms again.

She leaned into my embrace and turned to hug me.

"I am so glad you are home," she said, and started to tell me about some school event that Philip Jr. had planned that night.

I tried to listen, to be polite, but I just couldn't. I was still holding her there at the sink, and she was still chattering, but I heard none of it. Finally, I interrupted, just blurted it right out there: "How would you feel about having another baby?"

That left my dear wife speechless. That question might not have sounded all that strange for a young man to ask his wife. But coming from me, it was.

Few things in life was I more convinced of than that no one should have more than two children. Chrissie had heard me lecture for hours upon hours to anyone willing to listen. I had blessed anyone I shared a holiday meal, an airplane row—even some church gatherings—with, with my flawless, well-crafted argument.

It started like this: How could any couple possibly give enough love and attention to more than two? Then I would detail the costs: education, weddings, minivans instead of cars, larger houses, and more food and utilities. Looking back, I made a real pest of myself repeating my "logic" to my siblings (not that they listened; my sisters, Wendy and Louise, both have three children).

Chrissie and I already had two. Until this moment, we were done. This story was written, and no one knew it better than Chrissie. She stepped back and looked up at me with her face, her eyes searching mine. Had I gone mad? Was this a joke? Or perhaps simply an opening line for a night of romance? Words failed me. I didn't know how to begin explaining what had happened, how I could possibly be asking her about another baby. Silently, I reached in my pocket and pulled out the small black-and-white photo that I had gotten developed on my way home. "Andrew," I announced.

Chrissie didn't say a word. After drying her hands on her jeans, she took the photo out of my hand and stared at it, then looked back into my eyes, still searching for an explanation.

I didn't know how to verbalize what had happened. She looked down again at the little face staring back at her from the photo.

"Oh, yes," she said.

And that was that. A quiet peace fell over the room. She continued to look at the photo, holding it as carefully as she held her own children—too precious to hold, too dear to let go.

After a moment, she broke the silence. "How soon can I meet him?"

Life changed that day, from that very moment. We both became singly focused. The more I shared about our boy, the more restless and determined we both became. The Bible says you have not because you ask not. I started asking.

First, I called every name I had listed in my Rolodex—pastors and businessmen all around the country. Many of them had been friends of my dad's for decades; others were new friends whom I had ministered to in their churches, whose lost loved ones I had prayed for, or whom I had met in ministry somewhere along the way.

From that moment on, every conversation revolved around Andrew. "It's 7:00 in the morning there now; he'll just be waking up. Oh, I pray they have some cereal to give him." "I got a call from Pastor So-and-So with a thousand dollars; we only need eight hundred dollars more to buy two plane tickets to go see Andrew."

We prayed for him like nothing before. We prayed as a couple. We prayed as a family. The children were excited at the thought of having a little brother. While we didn't want to get their hopes up, we wanted them to be praying, for them to be part of the miracle. I prayed from the time I woke up until my last thought crossed my mind and I fell into sleep at night.

Andrew. My son. Our son.

"Lord, keep him safe until we can claim him as our own. Let no harm come to him," I prayed all night and day.

Every day was agony. We had no control or information about what was happening to him. He was only ours in our hearts, but he had filled our hearts so much; he was part of our every breath.

The days turned to weeks; the weeks to months. Only seeing the steady flow of money coming in kept me sane. I knew God was in control. I knew He had perfect timing. But it was maddening!

One of my trips for the ministry took me to Greenville, South Carolina, to a ministry run by Jimmy and Joanne Thompson. They were an amazing couple and force of God; two people God chose out of very ordinary beginnings to do extraordinary things for the kingdom.

What had started as a small church was now an outreach that included a publishing/printing firm and a twenty-four-hour Christian television network.

They shared my passion for orphans, especially those in Romania. When I was a guest there, I met a woman who pressed a folded piece of paper into my hand.

"Contact my friend Daniela when you get back to Romania," she said. "She helped a friend of mine from Canada adopt. She knows all the ropes and will gladly help you."

Thanking her, I tucked the paper safely into my wallet. The Lord knew I needed all the help I could get.

Chapter 7
The Journey for Andrew

Months later, we finally had enough money to start our journey back to Andrew. Chrissie talked like a nervous schoolgirl on the flight over, fretting about the bed she set up for him at home and the new toys she had in her luggage. But once the plane landed, she grew quiet.

I knew my girl well enough to know she was in deep conversation with the Lord. Part of her was worried, unsure of the challenges we might face; part of her was filled with silly fears that Andrew might not like her.

After a restless flight to Vienna and more than six hours of driving across three countries, Chrissie and I slowly pulled into the parking lot of a small motel in Arad, Romania.

Before leaving Alabama, we'd been able to contact the woman whose name had been given to us—Daniela—to see what help she could give us. She was very pleasant on the phone and readily agreed to travel with us to find Andrew's birth mother and help us make the boy our own.

As we pulled into the motel parking lot, I saw a woman standing off to the side of the building where we had planned to meet. She was our only connection, and I had faith that she would be a great help.

Though I was happy to see her, her appearance startled me. I'm not sure what I expected, but she was perhaps thirty, with a cold, harsh look about her. She was wearing skintight jeans—uncommon behind the previous Iron Curtain—and wore her long brown hair pulled back in a severe ponytail, with huge gold hoops hanging from her ears.

I had no reason to judge her on her appearance alone, but a flood of disappointment washed over me. It was scary to admit to myself how much hope I was pinning on this rough-looking woman. But at that point, I had no other choice. She was the only plan I had.

We exchanged hellos. After checking in to the motel, we mapped out our game plan for the next day. She sounded knowledgeable and bright. Pushing my fear aside, we set a time to meet her in the morning and wished her a good night.

After a fitful night of sleep, I awoke the next morning totally disoriented. My stomach grumbled impatiently as I momentarily waited for Chrissie to bring me my breakfast, as she did every morning. What would she make today? Perhaps poached eggs? Maybe a slab or two of ham? Or better yet, a steaming stack of pancakes?

But as I opened my eyes and the small, dreary motel room came into focus, I finally realized where I was and what I was doing there. Andrew's face came flooding back to me, my thoughts of breakfast forgotten immediately.

From the bathroom, I could hear Chrissie's voice in the shower. I couldn't tell if she was praying, singing, or talking to herself. But I knew from her tone that with every breath she took, she was becoming more determined and more ready for the battles ahead.

I wished I felt the same way. The challenges of adopting this child were going to be great. Unless we were successful in adopting him— and quickly—we would lose him forever. We couldn't let that happen. As I sat on the edge of the lumpy gray bed, I began to pray, my soul crying out at the thought of the boy staying even one more day where he was now.

Soon after, I felt the Holy Spirit begin to stir. My prayer of sadness became a prayer of hope, a hope so strong that it made no sense at all in the flesh. With my hands clasped together, I began to pray for the people we would meet along our path that day and in the days to come. I prayed for those people who could help us, those people whose names I didn't know, those people with whom we needed to share our goal: making this boy our own. I didn't know the names or even the titles of the government workers whose grace and assistance we needed, but God did.

I prayed for Andrew's birth mother, that she would see the love we had for her son, that she would allow us to become his family. I prayed for the woman with the paperwork at the orphanage, that her heart would be moved, that she would be given the wisdom to help and a passion to see this done. I prayed for the woman changing Andrew's diapers, for kindness, an extra measure of care. I prayed for Daniela, that she would be able to help us. I prayed that God would help us show this boy love, real love, starting today.

My wife came out of the shower, smiling at me in a way that melted my heart, her blonde hair hidden under the threadbare towel. She was my partner in all things. I never felt stronger than when she was by my side. She was the greatest gift God had ever given me in this world.

"Let's go get our boy," she said without a hint of doubt or fear.

I suddenly felt a sense of urgency and headed for the shower. It was time. God was moving in my heart, and I knew He was moving in others', too.

Soon after, with Daniela directing us, we settled in for the ride to the city where both Andrew and his birth mother would be found. We were quickly through a half-dozen roundabouts and out of the city. The full sun was bright in the sky. Though the roads were rough, we rode in comfortable silence.

A dull, low scream behind me interrupted the quiet, and I instinctively hit the brakes and turned my head toward the sound.

"Daniela!" I shouted, quickly pulling off to the side of the road. "What on earth? Are you okay? What is wrong?"

Her eyes were closed, her arms wrapped around her waist, and still she moaned. Finally, she spoke. "I am pregnant," she admitted. "It is just cramps. Bad ones. Next week I am going to have an abortion. I'll be fine. Keep driving."

An abortion? This woman who I was told was helping rescue babies—like my Andrew—was planning to kill her own? Who was this woman in my car? What was I supposed to do now?

Her pains continued, and I couldn't ignore her screams.

I quickly found a gas station, and Chrissie led Daniela to the bathroom, half carrying her across the parking lot. Soon after, ten minutes had passed. Then twenty. Forty-five minutes had passed when the women finally returned, and I got back in the car.

When I saw that she had stretched across the backseat and appeared to be napping, I increased the speed and tried not to think about how much hope we had pinned on her.

An hour later, we arrived at the university that Dana, Andrew's birth mother, attended. Daniela had pulled herself together. Leaving us in the car, she went to find Dana.

The wait for her return was unbearable. I wanted to cry; I wanted to laugh; I wanted to pee; I wanted to do everything all at once. My nerves were so raw. I was about to meet a stranger who held the power to grant me the greatest desire of my heart—Andrew—**or tear him away from us forever. She alone would validate what I had heard from God, that he was my son.**

Finally, we saw Daniela and Dana crossing the parking lot. When they reached the car, Dana immediately burst into tears. She couldn't look at me. The flood of emotions rattled me, but I pressed on.

After introducing myself, I turned to Chrissie. "Hi, I'm Philip," I stammered. "This is my wife, Chrissie, and we love your son."

Before I said another word, she asked us to take her to meet her boyfriend. It was clear that she could not face this conversation alone.

We found him across town as he was coming out of the sports complex where he played on the Romanian handball team. Dana jumped out of the car and ran to him, and I could tell that she was describing us without really knowing who we are or what she was supposed to do. Eventually, he joined us in the car.

Back at Dana's dorm, we all got to know one another. We learned that while he wasn't Andrew's biological father, he loved Dana and the child very much, and he was fiercely protective of them; I could tell he wasn't too keen on us.

I asked Dana to share what had happened, how her child had come to live in an orphanage. Her story was one of the saddest I had ever heard. As she spoke, tears poured down her cheeks.

Dana, a short young lady with dark hair and sad eyes, was only a teen when she fell hard for a good-looking, fast-talking young man whom she met at the university. Their courtship had developed from stolen kisses to dreams of the future.

But when Dana found out she was pregnant, everything turned sour. He did not want a baby; he was not ready for responsibility. He held her hand, looked into her eyes, and promised to help "take care of the problem." She would have an abortion. It was not up for discussion; it was a directive. He knew of a clinic on the other side of town; all they needed to do was get their hands on some money before her pregnancy moved into the second trimester, when an abortion would cost more.

Neither was working, so they had very little money to get by. Finally, Dana had an idea. She had one piece of jewelry that was precious to her. With tears in her eyes, she handed her delicate gold bracelet to her boyfriend to sell for the money they needed. He took it from her hand, kissed her on the cheek, and promised to call the next day to make the necessary plans and appointments.

It was the last she ever heard from him. Friends said he sold the bracelet and headed straight for the sunny beaches on the other side of the country.

Dana was all alone. Fear ruled her life. She was scared her mother would discover her pregnancy and take her out of the university. She ate little, slept little, and silently begged a god she didn't know for it all just to go away.

It was an unusually warm fall day when she went into labor on the 21st of September. With no other options, she walked two miles to the nearest hospital. Alone. There, she was turned away because she had no money.

"You have to go to the hospital for the poor," she was told.

Alone again, she walked across town while her labor progressed, resting at bus stops and park benches with each contraction. She was in the middle of a bustling city, in midday, but either no one noticed her pain, or no one cared.

She walked for another three miles before she finally saw the hospital in the distance. The sun was going down. Sweat poured off her swollen body. Her shoes were stained and wet from when her water had broken. She had eaten nothing in more than twenty-four hours, and the contractions were then less than a minute apart.

To her horror, she was told by a hard looking and sounding woman, "We are full. Every bed is taken." Dana met the woman's words with a loud groan, doubling over in front of her desk.

"Help me," Dana gasped through her clenched teeth. "Please. My baby is coming."

As workers scrambled to get her into a wheelchair and down the crowded hall to the delivery room, Dana collapsed. Almost as soon as they had her undressed, the baby's head crowned. A nurse cursed, her planned lunch suddenly canceled.

Silently, the doctor and his team went about their work. Not one word of comfort or encouragement was wasted on this poor young woman.

Andrew was born and let out a thin murmur instead of a lofty cry. Pulling off his gloves with a snap, the doctor headed for the door, with one of the nurses following behind with Andrew in her arms.

Dana was left all alone.

Twenty minutes later, an orderly came to remove her from the delivery room, just as she was starting to doze off. She was taken to a small dirty room at the end of the hallway.

There, Dana was forced to share not just a room, but also a bed with another patient. Her bedmate was a gypsy, a class of society that was deeply despised in Romania. But what choice did she have?

Dana bit back any protest she had, passed out from exhaustion, and slept for most of the next day.

Dana woke up cramped, hungry, and scared. The hospital did not provide food for its patients, and there was no one to bring Dana anything to eat. When the gypsy woman had her fill of what little food her family brought her, she, in her kindness, shared it with Dana.

Hours passed. Dana knew that the hospital would not keep her much longer, and she had nowhere to go. She thought about her options. There were no close friends or extended family members who would take in her and the baby. She didn't even have a dollar to her name.

And then there was her mother. Strict, judgmental, ruling their house with an iron fist. There was no way her mother would open her home to the baby; Dana would be lucky if her mother even took her back!

Soon, her exhaustion overcame her racing mind, and Dana drifted off to sleep. When she awoke again, a nurse with a clipboard was standing at her bedside.

"What time will your ride be picking you and the baby up?" she asked. "The latest you can stay is 2:00 p.m."

Dana glanced at the clock on the far wall. It was already 10:00 in the morning. After waiting as long as she could, she called her mom and told her the truth through fits of tears, begging for her help. In no time, Dana's mother arrived with an empty paper bag and a grim look on her face. She never asked to see the baby, never asked about her daughter's healing, just quickly found her way around the room, loaded Dana's clothes and shoes into the bag, and headed for the door.

Before she left, she announced, "When you are ready to sign that baby over to the state, I'll give you back your clothes."

By then, it was already 1:00 in the afternoon. Dana had nothing to wear but the soiled hospital gown she had on, not even a pair of socks. She had one hour to make a decision that would affect her and her baby for the rest of their lives.

Andrew became a ward of the bankrupt country of Romania, a so-called "economic orphan," with parents alive but unable to care for him. He was one of thousands and thousands of hopeless orphans.

When Dana stopped telling her story, I cleared my throat and started to ask the most difficult question I have ever asked. How does one even begin to ask a mother to give her child away forever to total strangers who live half a world away?

"Dana," I said softly, "your story breaks my heart. I know you love your baby more than life itself."

Dropping her head to her chest, Dana stared down at the floor, refusing to look in my direction.

"Chrissie and I love him, too. I know it sounds crazy, but we love him like he is our own. Ever since I met him a few months ago, he is all I think about, pray about. I want to give him a life, a real future.

"We live in America. We have two children who would love to have him as their little brother. He'll never be without. We will raise him to know the Lord, give him a good education, and love him with all our hearts. Would you consider allowing us to adopt your son?"

The room grew quiet; only the faint sounds of traffic outside evaded the silence. I started to say more, but I stopped myself. A few moments passed, and I realized I was holding my breath. A prayer escaped my heart, "Please, Lord, don't let her ask for any money." Even as tightly as my heart was wrapped around this boy, I knew that it was vitally important that one day, as this boy's father, I would be able to look him in his eyes and tell him without a shadow of a doubt that his mother had given him up out of her great love for him and not for any other reason. I could never have Andrew think his mother sold him for a fistful of money, or worse, that I bought him with a fistful of money.

Little did I know at the time, Dana had been offered $5,000 by another couple for the boy only weeks before. Despite her abject poverty, she decided to turn the couple down. "I didn't have a good feeling," Dana admitted later, thinking about that offer.

We talked for hours. Dana asked about our family, our house, and our children. I shared about my ministry, how I had come to meet her son, and our deep love for him.

Finally, Dana dropped her head to her chest as tears began to fall.

Wiping at them with the back of her hand, she tried to smile.

"Yes, I think you would be good for my boy," she said, her voice cracking. "Very good."

With that, Dana followed us down the three flights of stairs to the car below with Daniela. I wanted to sing, to shout, but I contained myself by catching Chrissie's eye. They were ready to help us make Andrew our own!

After spending another night at the motel in Arad, we picked up Dana and Daniela to start the wheels in motion. The twenty-minute drive from Dana's dormitory to the orphanage seemed to take hours. Finally, we drove down the little alley to the building where Andrew and the other children were housed.

It was another warm fall day with a bright sun against the bluest sky I have ever seen. After parking, Dana headed into the building in search of Andrew. The rest of us followed the chain-link fence surrounding the building, glancing at the yard, which was nothing more than a barren patch of dirt— without a single blade of grass and with no toys, no benches. After realizing that Andrew was not inside, Dana came back and joined us in the yard.

We found all the children sitting outside on tattered blankets, making games of throwing the colored leaves up into the air and watching them dance to the ground.

The children were laughing. Imagine that these orphans who had nothing were laughing at the pleasure of a few fall leaves floating through into the wind. I had to chuckle at their joy. But I quickly noticed that Andrew wasn't among them. I scanned the grounds, anxious to find my boy.

Finally, Dana and I spotted him at the same time on the other side of the yard. A blue wool cap was pulled tightly down on his head, and he stared off into the distance, not seeming to notice anything around him. He sat alone next to a rusty pipe, with no leaves with which to play.

I grabbed Chrissie's arm and pointed, then pulled her along with me toward him, my heart pounding. His blank face continued staring off into the distance as we approached. I stood beside him, and after a moment, he looked up.

Those green eyes melted me in an instant. I just wanted to hold him, wrap my arms around him. I wanted to take him to the car, to a plane, and to Alabama, where he belonged. My son. He was my son.

Dana reached down, pulled Andrew into her arms, and turned to introduce him to Chrissie.

Chrissie pulled off the blue cap as she took the boy into her arms. My heart dropped. They had shaved him bald! Every hair on my boy's sweet head was gone. It was gone! Why had they done this to my Andrew?

Tenderly, Chrissie rubbed his naked little head, and as she held him for the first time, her face had the same glow as when she delivered our two children. In her heart, at that moment, in that filthy place, Andrew was born.

I watched as she placed one of her small hands on each side of his face, the photo on our refrigerator coming to life in her arms. He blinked and slowly turned his face to hers. Time froze. His piercing green eyes focused on her face, her hair, and finally her eyes.

And then Andrew did something breathtaking. He smiled.

This hungry, bald, abandoned boy smiled, not at the woman who had given birth to him, but at the woman who was in an instant his mother. As mother and child got to know each other, I sat down inside with the orphanage worker I had met before. I had left her money—one hundred dollars, three months' wages—and begged her to promise that she would find answers for me to confirm that he could be adopted. My efforts had gotten me nowhere, so I'd stopped calling her a few months before. I knew that I would make no real progress until I was physically in the country again.

When I walked in, she glanced up and then back down at her paperwork. Then she looked again, startled, like she had seen a ghost.

"Mr. Cameron, hello," she said. Glancing behind me, her face registered surprise at the sight of Dana. "I did not expect you."

"What have you learned about the boy?" I asked without the usual pleasantries. "My wife and I are here with his birth mother to do whatever is required to adopt him and take him back to the States. We have her permission; she'll sign anything she needs to. What can you tell me?"

The woman looked pale, nervous.

"We thought . . . I thought . . . well, it's just that Andrew is scheduled to be reassigned on . . ." Her voice trailed as she checked her calendar.

"Yes, right here. In three weeks, he will be picked up and transferred to another orphanage."

The woman was talking about my boy like he was a UPS package! Someone else's UPS package! Picked up? Transferred? Another facility? Where? Why? The questions rattled in my brain faster than I could process them, much less get them out.

"You see, Mr. Cameron, the boy turned four last Monday. That is the cutoff age at this institution. We are preparing him to be moved, and," she said as she shuffled through her papers, "there is no way to help you. There is nothing here about where he is going, only what date and time he is to be picked up, October 21 at 11:00 a.m."

How could she be telling me that they were taking Andrew away to God knows where and I couldn't do a single thing about it?

"There is no way," she repeated. "No way."

This boy meant nothing to her, and I meant even less. She was an agent of the government, one of the seemingly countless faceless, heartless souls who spent their days mindlessly following rules and orders. The boy's fate had been dictated by the strike of a pen. Done. Finished.

The silence between us grew awkward. I cleared my throat and shifted in my seat.

"Excuse me," I finally said. "I am not giving up. That is my boy. I didn't come halfway around the world to be turned away like this."

I stopped talking, my mind racing ahead. She was the only link I had to the people making the decision. Even with Dana's permission to take the boy, I still could do nothing. Andrew could be lost forever in the bowels of the Romania orphan system.

"But you didn't lose him," the Lord spoke to my rapidly beating heart. "He is here. You are here. I am here." As His words soothed my spirit, the words of a praise song I'd sung all my life came into my heart:

> I know the Lord will make a way for me.
> I know the Lord will make a way for me.
> If I live a holy life, shun the wrong, and do the right.
> I know the Lord will make a way for me.

With renewed faith that God would indeed make a way for me, I demanded to see someone in charge. Less than an hour later, we stood in front of yet another worker, a tall blonde supervisor with the charm of a rabid pit bull.

"Have a seat," she motioned as she launched into her speech. "Mr. Cameron, these children are in our care. We can't let just anyone take them. We'd have to have a government official grant permission for such a thing," she said as she pushed back her chair and stood. "Only the mayor himself could grant that."

Silence filled the room. Chrissie took my hand and squeezed it. She didn't have to tell me what she was thinking. I could tell by the look on her face.

"Thank you so much for all your help," I said as I glanced down at the papers the woman had given me. "Could you kindly direct me to the mayor's office?"

Our trip to the mayor's office—a small, ugly, two-floor building with tiny windows—was my next glimpse into the dysfunctional government that was now running this post-Soviet country. There was no money to provide the people with even the most basic services that they'd had in the past. Mother Russia no longer backed the country's power and control, so the government sought to hang onto power through intimidation and rudeness. And it was darn good at it.

Inside, a young woman, dressed in the same dull brown as her surroundings, sat at a metal desk in the foyer. As we walked up to her desk, she ignored us as she continued to rapidly read through the stack of papers on her desk.

Minutes went by. Chrissie cleared her throat. I rattled the car keys, tapped my foot on the tile floor. Dana stood behind us, and Daniela went off in search of a ladies' room. The woman kept reading, stopping only to pick up a pencil and mark a few words in the margin. Finally, she turned to what looked like the last page, finished it, filed it, and then looked up with a face filled with boredom.

"Yes?" she asked.

"We're here to see the mayor," I said. "We've traveled a very long way to get here."

When it was clear that the distance we'd traveled did not impress her, I told her that the fate of a small orphan child rested in our hands and of the supposed wealth we had as Americans. I felt like Dorothy and the Scarecrow outside the gate of the Emerald City.

There was no way, she said, that we would be allowed to see the mayor.

Her words hung in the air: No way. No way.

With that, she spun around in her chair until her back was facing us and started digging through a tall beige filing cabinet.

I stared at the back of her head, and we waited. Again, the minutes passed by. Finally, she turned, surprised to see us still standing there.

Over the next four hours, I talked my way not only past her, but also past several other higher levels of secretaries and managers. Finally, I sat down with the man himself—the mayor of this seemingly godforsaken city—and explained through an interpreter what I wanted to do.

I saw heads shaking, people frowning, and heard the words, "No way," echoing in my head, yet still in my heart I heard, "I know the Lord will make a way for me."

Hours later, through the grace and providence of God, I had a note in my hand—permission to take Andrew out of the orphanage!

Chrissie and I hurried to the car before the mayor could change his mind. I peeled out of the parking lot, gravel flying and my wife laughing. Dana sat stoically behind us, wide-eyed.

We had it; we had permission to take the boy! We were one step closer to claiming this child as our own, against all odds! I'm not sure if there were speed limits in Romania, but if there were, we broke every one of them getting back to the orphanage and getting Andrew back in our arms.

Less than thirty minutes later, we were walking past a very shocked orphanage worker as she read the permission slip one more time. She didn't think we'd ever get the mayor to sign off on us taking the boy out—why should he? But as we walked out with Andrew in our arms, that song danced across my heart again:

> I know the Lord will make a way for me.
> I know the Lord will make a way for me.
> If I live a holy life, shun the wrong, and do the right.
> I know the Lord will make a way for me.

Chapter 8
No Way

There were no car seats in Romania then (in fact, I doubt many people have them now), so Chrissie climbed into the front seat beside me with Andrew in her arms. Dana and Daniela climbed into the back.

Wide-eyed, Andrew looked around the car in awe, and it suddenly occurred to me that this poor child had never been anywhere but in the orphanage or the yard, and he certainly had no concept of what a car was. He didn't know us, didn't understand a word we said. His eyes were wide like saucers, not from fear, but from curiosity.

As I started the car, music from the radio filled the air. At once Andrew began bouncing up and down to the tune, so excited that I was afraid he would hurt himself. Puzzled by the sound, he bent down and put his ear to the speaker, rocking his bald head to the beat. He had never heard music before.

His smile was beyond anything I can put into words. My heart was so full I thought I would burst. He was here, right here, in the car with us! What a miracle!

Thanking God, I put the car in reverse and backed out of the drive. Andrew continued to bounce to the music, and Chrissie reached to the back of the car and pulled out a two-liter bottle of Pepsi. Before she could get a cup or try to communicate and ask if he was thirsty, Andrew grabbed the huge bottle and put it to his lips.

Chrissie and I watched, dumbfounded. This tiny boy drank the entire bottle in a matter of minutes, stopping only once for air. I had never seen anything like it!

Then I remembered what one of the workers told me: The children were given only a tiny bit of water each day so they would not need to urinate very often. The less urine, the fewer diaper changes or trips to the potty. Either of these outcomes meant less work for the caretakers. This poor child had been dehydrated his entire life. I shook my head at the thought, the inhumanity, and started down the road.

My mind wandered as we started aimlessly down the street. A motel room would cost at least seventy dollars, and I had maybe twenty-five dollars left. How could that motel get away with charging seventy dollars a night for such a dirty little room?

"It's because we are Americans," I reminded myself.

Rich Americans—I laughed aloud at the thought. So rich that we were homeless. It just wasn't fair. If we had been guests of a local company or church, I knew the motel would only charge three dollars. But since we were Americans . . .

Suddenly, everything became clear. A church was the only place in town where I knew anyone—the very church that my dad and I had stopped at the first time we came to Romania six months before. We had loaded all of our food, all the medicine, blankets, and formula into its warehouse. By the time the church "discovered" the orphanage a stone's throw away, everything was gone. The church had given it to its own starving people.

I looked around for a place to turn around. Surely the church would help. It would cost it nothing to book the motel—we could pay for it; we just needed it booked in the church's name.

I smiled at the beauty of the plan. It was perfect. God was in control. I put a bit more pressure on the accelerator, and twenty minutes later we were pulling up outside the familiar building. The truth was, I hated to ask the church for anything, a seed of resentment still in my soul over what had happened.

I looked at Andrew's face, the picture of an angel, then at Chrissie, Daniela and Dana. I had no choice. I was desperate—too desperate to let my ego stand in the way.

I left the others in the car and was relieved to find the church door unlocked.

"Hello," I called, "anyone here?" My voice echoed down the empty halls. I walked across the parking lot, over to the warehouse, the "scene of the crime." To my relief, there were a few workers. I didn't know any of their names, but I recognized a few of the faces. After taking a deep breath, I started making my case:

"My name is Philip Cameron. I live in America and was just here a few months ago. Maybe you remember," I said. "We brought a huge tractor-trailer filled with food and supplies. I was a rich man that day, and I had many things to give your people."

"Today I have nothing. I have nowhere to stay. My wife is waiting for me in the car with a little boy we are trying to adopt. If the church would book us a motel room—which we would gladly pay for—it would only cost three dollars a night. But if I book it, they charge seventy dollars. I am exhausted. I have no money. Please, can you help me?"

The men looked at one another. It was easy to tell that they'd understood enough of what I said to know they wanted no part of it. Why would they help me? I had nothing to give them.

No one would look at me, each shaking his head in a silent, "Sorry, but no." I took Andrew's hand; Chrissie held the other. We were beaten, we'd have to put Andrew back in the orphanage.

I started to protest, when a voice boomed from behind me. "Philip Cameron!"

Turning, I was met with the biggest, most welcome smile I have ever seen. It was Ion, the man I had met a year before who asked for the James Dobson books.

"Thanks for the books," he said, grabbing me in a bear hug. "You have no idea what a blessing they have been to the ministry."

He stood there staring at me like I was a returning hero. "What brings you back here, brother?"

I motioned for him to follow me outside, out of the earshot of the others. After finding a few chairs for us to sit in, I told him all that had happened from the time we left the goods at the church to the many legal dead ends we'd faced in trying to adopt Andrew.

"My friend, I am out of money and out of ideas," I said. "We have no place to stay and less than a quarter of a tank of gas. I have hit a wall. Can you help me? Do you know any way to help us? Anyone?"

I looked at him, and he looked, well, embarrassed.

"Ion? What are you thinking? You know someone, don't you? Tell me, please!"

He cleared his throat, "Philip, I am the only Christian in my family. I share my faith every chance I get, but so far, nothing. My sister . . . well, she is the mistress of the vice president of the court."

The enormity of his words washed over me, and my heart leaped in anticipation of what he would say next.

"I am not sure why the church will not help you book a room, but I have a better idea," he continued. "I have a flat not far from here. It's small, but my wife and I can go and stay with my in-laws, and you can use it as home base for a few days. I'll take you to meet my sister, and then we can go to my home. I can't promise my sister will agree to help, but it is worth a try."

The ride across town seemed endless (as nearly all of the trips had). I was anxious to meet Ion's sister, hopeful that she would be able to help us. As she came down to meet us at the car, I was immediately struck by her presence. She had an hourglass figure in a Mae West kind of way. Her long dark hair fell over her pale shoulders in waves, setting off her rich brown eyes. Her arms were long and thin; her nails painted a bright red. Her voice was deep and throaty; her manner, almost abrasive. Everything about this woman screamed for attention and control. She dressed unlike anyone I had seen in Romania. In a world where everyone wore black and brown, her dress was a vivid shade of blue, tight, and cinched at the waist with a large leather belt. She stood perhaps five feet, five inches in her tall heels and may very well have been wearing the only pair of panty hose in Eastern Europe.

As soon as we told her our story, Ion's sister began to cry.

"I will do whatever I can to help you," she said, with Ion translating. "Meet me tomorrow morning at the courthouse, and I will make it so the vice president of the court will see you; he will not say no to me."

The next morning, we arrived at the court. Hundreds of people lined the halls. We followed behind Ion's sister as if we were lost puppies, not knowing where we were going. After what seemed like hours, she opened the big leather padded door at the end of the hallway and walked in. Ignoring the two secretaries who sat guarding the inner office, she flung open another door, unannounced.

There sat Cristian Dacu, vice president of the court. I had no idea what he would say, how he would react. I stood behind Ion's sister, not understanding a word she was saying to him. I was surprised when he looked over his high desk and asked, in perfectly clear English, where in Alabama I was from.

After listening to our story, he said, "Normally, there is a six-week waiting period for the mother. Do you think she would allow that to be put aside?"

"I know she would, yes."

"Come back on Thursday at 2:00," he said. "The boy will need his birth certificate, too."

Less than an hour later, we returned to Ion's tiny flat. Ion's wife made us a cabbage-and-pork soup and served it with thick slices of crusty bread. I ate like a man spared from execution. Finally, we had hope. We had a plan. We had help. I couldn't stop thanking the Lord, praising Him. I couldn't stop smiling at my pretty wife, tickling that boy who would soon be mine.

Chapter 9
The End of the Line

When Chrissie, Daniela, and I arrived at Ion's that night, I placed a call to my office in America. I had a handful of dedicated, hardworking staff members—low paid, but loyal to the core. "I need you to overnight us some more money," I said as soon as Lisa answered. "We've gone through almost everything we have, and I have no idea how long we'll be here."

"Well, I don't know what to tell you," she stammered. "Things aren't good here either. I'm not sure what we can scrape together to send to you. Honestly, we are about at the end of the line. I'm not sure how we are going to survive this."

See, there was a problem, and it was a big one: If I was not preaching in churches every Sunday, the ministry didn't have any income. These trips to Romania were not exactly in our budget, nor was the loss of income while I was away. I had been gone a week, with our return nowhere in sight, and I was down to the last few dollars in my pocket. I needed them to send money right away.

"How bad is it?" I asked, but the truth was I knew before she said a word.

"Things are pretty grim around here," Lisa sighed. "I wasn't able to make payroll yesterday because the money just isn't there. I gave everyone a few dollars for groceries and gas, but it won't last long. You didn't take your last paycheck, remember, so there isn't even money in your account to pay your mortgage or anything else. I am hoping they don't turn off the lights."

Static filled the line as she fell silent.

Daniela had offered for us to stay with her and her mom in Bucharest, and we had no choice but to accept. Frankly, up until this point, she had been useless beyond some simple translations. I didn't trust her, didn't like her, and not simply because I was judging her for her planned abortion; everything about her seemed fake. I wanted to get away from her, but I had little choice.

Closing my eyes, I began to pray silently. It was all starting to look impossible, yet I knew what the Lord was telling me to do. Lisa promised to make a few calls and do the best she could, but she sounded utterly defeated. I didn't have the words to encourage her and, after giving her Daniela's address to send the money to, ended the call as quickly as I could.

In an effort to forget the call, I tried to focus on the day ahead. It was time to pay a visit to Dana's mother. I was more nervous about asking her for Andrew's birth certificate than I had been about meeting Dana. Dana told us story after story of her mother, and I knew that she had no love for Andrew, that she had no compassion for her daughter. She refused to even meet Andrew when he was born, and I knew that a woman who was capable of calling her own grandson a bastard was also capable of preventing us from taking him, just to spite Dana.

When we were let into the apartment, Dana was immediately led away by her mother to the kitchen, and I could hear her howling in tears through the thin walls. The woman said nothing to persuade Dana to keep Andrew, but her actions said it all. She came out of the kitchen and sat beside the boy, stroking his head, kissing his cheek. I knew if we stayed there, Dana would never let us take Andrew; her mother would persuade her to keep legal guardianship of him while he suffered in the orphanage.

I silently begged God not to let that happen. A clock on the mantel ticked loudly as the minutes passed. I could not understand anything being said between mother and daughter, but there was a peace that began to settle in the room, a presence that I could almost see. Finally, the older woman stood, shook her head, and walked out of the room. When she returned, she handed a small brown envelope to Dana, kissed Andrew's head, and disappeared back into the kitchen. We had the final document we needed!

The next day, we had a court session. As in every Communist court, there were five judges, dressed in robes, lording over the proceedings. Just seeing these formally attired men made my heart skip a beat. We had come so far. If they didn't give us permission to take Andrew, I would be forced to give up. They were the final rule in Romania; there was no court of appeals. There would be nowhere left to turn.

The whole process was a blur, as if I were watching it from afar, not taking part in it.

"The social study's waived?"

"Yes."

"Who is giving this baby up for adoption?"

Dana stood up. "I am. I am the child's mother."

"Who is accepting this child?"

Chrissie and I stood up. "We are." I looked over at Chrissie, and she was wearing a look of complete serenity.

"Lord Jesus," I prayed, "move against all odds on this situation."

Bang! The gavel came down; the vice president of the court was on his feet, and Ion's sister looked like the cat that swallowed the canary. Daniela smiled.

"He is yours," she said, smiling.

Chrissie and I jumped up and down, screaming with joy at the news that Andrew was our boy at last. Right there in the courtroom, I planted a big kiss on Chrissie's smiling face. I even managed to hug Daniela. Still beaming, I turned to hug Dana too.

The look on Dana's face was a strange mixture of sadness and happiness, confusion and realization. It dawned on me in that moment that this news meant the end for Dana and this boy. She was losing him forever. As long as he was in the orphanage, there was always a chance, however slim, that one day they would be a family. Now, all hope was gone.

We headed to the car, and Dana climbed onto the backseat. Daniela leaned against the door on her side. The sun had set and a dark stillness blanketed the car. No one said a word as I started down the street toward the edge of town and began the journey back to Dana's dorm.

Andrew was starting to tire and was snuggling into Chrissie's arms to sleep. Chrissie hugged the boy close then handed him back to Dana. As a mom, Chrissie was keenly aware that this was the last chance Dana would have to feel the warmth and joy of her child sleeping in her arms.

It seemed for a moment Andrew would relax and sleep in the back with her, but suddenly, he bolted for the front seat.

"Mommy!" he screamed, struggling to climb back into the front to Chrissie.

All week, we had been working with Andrew to bond Chrissie to him as his mother, and it had worked. I didn't hear Dana crying as the child settled back into Chrissie's lap to sleep, but I knew she was. How could she not be?

Chrissie and I were anxious to drop off Dana and head with Daniela to the embassy in Bucharest to get our son's passport and start our new lives. But at the same time, I was painfully aware of the anguish that every mile brought to the young girl behind me. One mile closer to our having the boy. One mile closer to her losing the boy.

With Chrissie and I being from one country, living in another, and adopting a toddler from a third, the next vital step was to get a passport for Andrew that would allow him out of Romania, through the countries in our path, and finally back home to America. If you have never traveled outside the United States, it is almost impossible to explain how important a passport is. That little booklet proves to authorities all over the world who you are, where you have been, and what permissions you have regarding entering and staying in other countries. Passports aren't given at birth, and people generally don't get them until they need to travel. Without a passport for the child, none of the hurdles we had overcome would matter. Andrew would be stuck in Romania.

Finally, we were back at Dana's dormitory parking lot. It was dark, with only a single streetlamp to help light the way. A burning pile of garbage cast a yellow glow over everything. I stopped the car, started to unload the few things Dana brought, and turned to say our good-byes.

"You will be good to the baby?" Dana asked as we stood behind the car. I nodded. Of course.

Chrissie handed Andrew back to her for a final hug. Sobbing, she rubbed his fuzzy head against her cheek, breathed in his sweet baby smell as if to engrave it on her heart. Again, we reassured her that we would love him and that he would never want for anything, and we promised a Christmas picture and update every year and that I would visit when I came back to Romania.

"Please take care of my baby," Dana said as she handed the child back to us. She quickly turned away from her only child, burying her head in her hands.

Wordlessly, Chrissie and I quickly jumped back in the car and started on our way.

I looked back as we drove away. I couldn't stop myself. Dana was crying uncontrollably on the pavement, clutching her stomach, the pain of losing her child too great to bear.

In that moment, I felt like a criminal. But again, I heard in my heart, "I know the Lord will make a way."

As the words of the song soothed my spirit, the dam of emotions within me burst. I was driving while sobbing hysterically. It was a miracle I didn't hit anyone or anything because I was completely on autopilot.

I didn't know north from south, east from west; all I knew was I had to put distance between Andrew's birth mother and us before I could relax in my spirit. I don't mean that harshly; I loved Dana. But my heart was so attached to Andrew. I just wanted him to be mine forever. Realizing I had not been paying attention and had no idea where we were, I heard myself pray out loud, "Lord, if I am headed the wrong way, will you let a fox run across the road?"

Now, mind you, in all my trips to Romania, I had never seen a fox in the road. Not once. Where this prayer came from, I had no idea.

A darting motion caught my eye. It was a small gray fox, its tail as long as its thin body. It started out, glared into my lights, then quickly passed in front of my car and disappeared into the woods on the other side of the road.

I grinned at Chrissie, did a quick U-turn, and headed out of town, with tears still wet on my face, but a grin as well.

After driving all night, we finally arrived at Daniela's the next morning, in the capital, Bucharest. I was exhausted from the trip, but also wired, a ball of nervous energy, anxious to move this process along.

The building she lived in was one of six in a sad complex of three-story buildings. We unloaded the car and followed her up the stairs, my mind suddenly fixated on the thought of a hot shower and a clean set of clothes.

Trash littered the stairway and halls, and an unpleasant smell permeated the building. Daniela turned her key into three different dead bolts and let us in with a series of clicks.

I looked around at the place she was living in with her mother. The floor was a dull vinyl, devoid of color, and I could just make out the faintest track of some floral pattern on the faded wallpaper. Where pictures had once hung there were only nails, and dog poop and hair littered the floor.

It seemed to be a main room with a tiny kitchenette off to the side and a bedroom in the back. A chipped bowl sat empty beside the sink, along with a box of what looked like breakfast cereal. As best I could tell, it was the only food in the house.

After dropping my bags near the door, I set off to find the bathroom, carefully skirting around the dog poop, which seemed to be everywhere. In the tiny flat, the bathroom wasn't hard to find, but it was the strangest I had ever seen. The room was small—so small that I could touch the wall in front of me, the wall behind me, and the wall to my right, all while sitting on the toilet.

Stranger still, the showerhead was mounted on the wall above the toilet, and the drain was at my feet. The entire room was the shower stall! I could have dealt with that okay, but there was no water. Apparently, water would get turned on from time to time, often in the middle of the night, and everyone would jump up, get a shower, fill the sink, and then go back to bed.

Since there was no water, I quickly gave up on the thought of a shower, and walked gingerly back to the living room, trying to avoid stepping in anything vile.

Daniela took what money I had left and went to the corner market to see if they had any eggs, meat, or bread—anything—to buy.

The apartment only had two small windows and two dimly lit lamps. Chrissie and I were assigned the one private bedroom, and I put on my pajamas and crawled into bed. After the few days we'd had, I thought going to bed would be easy, but I was wrong. At the end of the bed, Chrissie sat staring at me, bouncing Andrew in her arms.

"Aren't you coming to bed?" I asked, stifling a yawn.

"Philip Cameron, have you not noticed that this place is filthy? I bet she hasn't washed those sheets in years! Look! See that? Fleas! The bed is crawling with fleas!"

Ignoring Chrissie's complaints, I took the boy from her and leaned back. His skin was damp with sweat, and the smell of urine clung to him like a blanket. He peed all the time and had no control at all over his bowels. But I held him close and rocked him, feeling the fleas stinging my skin.

Suddenly, there was a knock on the door.

"Philip," Daniela's irritating voice came from the other side of the door. "You have a phone call." She threw the phone onto the floor, and I, on my hands and knees, searched for the handset.

A phone call? Who the heck knew where to find me?

"Hello?"

"Philip Cameron!" the familiar voice of an old friend came through the line. It was Bob D'Andrea, president of the Christian Television Network (CTN) in Clearwater, Florida.

"Philip, you are on the air! You were supposed to be here with us tonight."

I groaned inwardly. That appointment was one of the many that I had canceled to come and get Andrew.

"So," he said, "how are you doing?"

For a moment, I hesitated. I was raised to give a good report. After all, God is always in control. But the words of great news and high hopes were far from my lips.

"Brother Bob," I muttered, "things are bad. I am trying to adopt a baby in Romania, and while doors keep opening, there are so many of them. This is taking forever. The government is a nightmare. We have no gas for the car. I am out of money, so we can't afford a motel. I have no idea if we will even have supper tonight. There is no food."

A few minutes later, after I complained in even greater detail, we ended the call. I returned to the bedroom and climbed back into bed with the fleas.

Turning to Chrissie, I said, "Well, that is one program that I'll never have to worry about getting invited back to."

I rolled over. Somehow, I slept.

It was only later that I learned that as soon as I hung up, Bob looked directly into the television camera and talked to the people in his live audience, broadcasting all over Florida in real time.

"Friends, we have to pray, and we have to do something to help Philip and this little orphan boy. For the next twenty minutes, we are going to pray, and as we do, I am going to ask you to go to the phone and call in a gift. Every penny you give in the next twenty minutes will go directly to help Philip Cameron."

He prayed. The people gave. And $20,000 came in and saved my ministry and my house and allowed me to stay and fight the good fight for my boy. It was a miracle, but I slept without knowing it.

The next morning, I awoke with hope that we would be able to get a motel room and escape staying another night in that filthy dump.

Daniela's mother handed us a plate of food; apparently, she'd been able to get some bread and meat. I was too hungry and too broke not to eat a little of it.

As we ate, Daniela disappeared behind the closed door of the bedroom and then came out with a big smile on her face.

"Look," she said, "a package for you."

It was easy to tell it had already been opened. Inside, all I found was a note from Lisa, a handful of candy, and two dollars.

"Where is the rest of it?" I demanded.

Daniela looked bewildered. I wasn't stupid. Lisa had not sent me an overnight package with only two dollars in it!

I looked past Daniela long enough to see her mom pick up a piece of ham from the floor—dog poop, hair, and all—and place it on Chrissie's plate. Disgusted, I stood up. It was time to go. I'd sleep in the car before I'd spend another night with this con woman and her mother.

Turning to Chrissie, I quietly said, "Let's go. These people aren't helping us. They are stealing from us."

Not knowing how to get to the Embassy, we left Daniela and her mother behind. I could not stand to spend one more day with those women, and there was no way I was going to let them steal from me again.

Chapter 10
The Baby with No Country

Somehow, we found our way to the American Embassy. When we finally found the building after a few wrong turns and false starts, I let out a sigh of relief. I have always loved the sight of the American flag blowing in the breeze, but never more than at that moment, seeing it there marking the American embassy.

In that moment, it meant hope. People would understand English. They would share my concern for this child. We would not be alone in this fight anymore. My passport was my ticket to help, and I needed it desperately.

As I stepped inside the embassy, it was as though we had left Romania entirely. The floors were gleaming white with thick carpets. Impressive paintings hung on every wall. Glass vases filled with fresh flowers sat on massive wooden desks. Looking down at my wrinkled clothes and dull shoes, I suddenly felt very out of place.

"May I help you, sir?" the woman at the front desk said with a slight New England accent.

I stepped up to her desk, introduced myself, and explained, "We are here because my wife and I live in America, and we really need some help. We have green cards, but we are British citizens. This little boy, Andrew, is an orphan. We would like to take him back to Alabama."

The lady dropped her head and peered at me over her thick glasses. "Sir," she said with an air of disgust, "what are you doing here?"

"Pardon me?" I asked, confused.

"This is the American embassy," she said. Behind me I heard Chrissie start to cry.

"You are not American," the woman continued, as if we hadn't heard or understood her the first time. "You are British. I have no idea what you are doing here or what possessed you to think you can adopt a Romanian child. There is no way I can help. Good day, sir."

I was stunned. Everything about the woman had totally rattled me to the core. I was speechless, stunned, frozen in place.

Mustering up courage I didn't feel, I said, "You will see me again," and I turned on my heel, put my arm around Chrissie's tiny waist, and led her from the building.

By the time we got to the door, her body was heaving with sobs. I looked at her red face, wet with tears, those eyes I loved puffy from so little sleep. I heard in my heart: "I know the Lord will make a way."

I was overwhelmed by the gravity of the situation; we had come so far, overcome so many obstacles. All I could do was take our case down the street to the British Embassy and pray the Lord would pave the way. Moments later, another flag of red, white, and blue waved in the breeze—the British Union Jack—marking the building as property of my motherland.

Inside, the British embassy was as stately as the American, filled with good-looking men and women in their tailored suits. An L-shaped desk with the most modern Selectric typewriter I had ever seen sat in the foyer. A smart-looking woman was pulling a form out of her machine and turned to greet me as I approached.

Once again, I introduced myself and told her why I was there. I drew back, expecting some taunt or reprimand. Instead, the woman stood and extended her hand, "My name is Thelma. Just where in the UK are you folks from?"

Startled, I stammered a bit. "It's such a wee place, I doubt you have heard of it. Peterhead, Scotland. It's up—"

She cut me off. "Aye, I know exactly where Peterhead is; I grew up not far from there myself!"

For a moment we bantered back and forth like old friends, talking about the places we missed, foods you could only get back home, people we might have known in common. Just by hearing a kind voice, sharing a bit of home, I felt that hope was being rekindled. It was refreshing, like a cool drink of water.

Finally, Thelma noticed someone behind me waiting for her attention. "You will need to see my boss," she said, hurrying us along as she waved the next couple forward. "Her name is Christy Gordon-Rowe. She is tied up right now, but if you will have a seat, she'll be with you very soon."

Turning to Chrissie, I saw that her eyes were still clouded from crying. I could tell the slightest setback would cause her to melt into a puddle of fresh tears.

Suddenly, the halls echoed with the wailing of a grief-stricken woman. "No!" she cried. "You can't take him! He is mine! I have cared for him since the day he was born. If you won't give me the papers, I will smuggle him out of this godforsaken place!"

Hearing the raw pain in the woman's voice was all Chrissie could stand. As the details of her story poured out in torrents of tears and screams, it was clear that the British woman had more claim on her baby than we did on Andrew. Yet she was still being denied the right to take him to her home in Canada.

After excusing herself, Chrissie took Andrew to a bench in the back of the room while I waited for the meeting, feeling powerless and alone.

It was years before I learned what had happened when Chrissie sat down on that bench.

She dropped her face in her hands and began to weep uncontrollably. As she cried, her heart was too wounded to even pray. All hope was gone.

Her love for Andrew was so deep, so pure, and she couldn't imagine life without him. She couldn't imagine loving him so much and having to leave him in that orphanage again. As her sobs turned to silent tears, she felt the warmth of two hands on her shoulders, as if someone was standing behind her. Yet she was sitting with her back close to the wooden bench that she was sitting on. The hands were large, firm, reassuring. Chrissie gasped but was afraid to open her eyes. She was afraid that the feeling, the very real touch she felt on her shoulders, would disappear.

When she finally opened her eyes, no one was there—no one she could see, anyway. But she knew. She knew Jesus was with us and that Andrew would be our son.

Meanwhile, the esteemed Ms. Gordon-Rowe greeted me. Stone-faced and hard, she didn't even have to open her mouth before I knew she would not be helping us.

She talked to me as if I were a dim-witted boy. "Mr. Cameron, I don't know what made you think we could help. You live in America. The baby is Romanian. There is nothing I can do for you."

And without as much as a good-bye, she walked back to her office and closed the door with a thud.

I was crestfallen. I stood frozen in my tracks. It was the end of the road—we'd have to leave him here, twelve hours away from the orphanage. Then I thought of Chrissie. She was already a mess. How would she handle one more rejection, one more dead end?

Andrew was still fast asleep as I walked up. Looking at Chrissie, I could tell something had changed, that she had changed. There was a sparkle in her eyes I had not seen in days. I hated to tell her the news and spoil her mood, but I had no choice.

"Chrissie, they can't help us either," I started. "We live in America."

"That's okay, we have all the help we need," Chrissie said with a boldness that rocked me back on my heels. She grabbed the baby buggy, and we headed to the car. We didn't say a word as we loaded the car, but I could make out the faintest of tunes as my wife folded up the buggy for the truck. Was she humming the tune of "I Know the Lord Will Make a Way"?

The British embassy rejected us; we weren't living in Britain at the time, so it had no say in the American matters. And the American embassy wouldn't even let us in anymore because we weren't American citizens. All we had were our American green cards and Andrew with his Romanian birth certificate. We were at a loss.

But Chrissie's sudden calmness centered me. Moments before, my thoughts had drifted to what it would be like, feel like, to take Andrew back to the orphanage, fly home, and start over. I decided to apply for a Romanian passport. He'd need one. The man at the passport office took my gift, a packet of cigarettes, and told me to come back the next day. It was waiting for us at 9:00 the next day. I decided to try the British Consulate one more time. Thelma was surprised to see us. I held up Andrew's red Romanian passport. "Thelma, we got this passport. He is now Andrew Cameron." Thelma stood up. She couldn't speak. Finally, she blurted out "What have you done? What have you done? He is neither Romanian, Scottish or American. He has your name but no country." "Thelma, he is mine. I want to see the consular again." Thelma left holding Andrew's passport. It seemed like ages. "Come with me." I couldn't read her at all. Soon I was sitting across the desk looking Cristy Gordon-Rowe face to face. Her elbows leaned on the arms of her chair. "So you want a visa to take your boy to

Scotland?" Yes. I thought that if we got Andrew there with my mom and dad we could fight for his US visa and he at least would be safe.

Now I knew better. In spite of all the setbacks we had faced, God was in control. The only thing I knew to do was drive to Vienna in preparation of our return to America and trust that He would make a way for us to take Andrew home with us.

We arrived in Vienna that afternoon at twenty minutes to four. I knew it was getting late, and I told Chrissie, "Let's go to the American embassy. I know it didn't work in Romania, but let's give it another shot."

The minute the words came out of my mouth, it occurred to me that we wanted to go to the Marriott. To this day, I don't know how I knew that, but the urging in my spirit was clear. It turned out that the American embassy was on the fourth floor of the same building that housed the Marriott.

Despite this happy coincidence, we had no idea what to expect as we walked up to the embassy. Would they be able to help us, or would they just turn us away like the embassies in Romania had? Would they even let us in?

We got inside and explained our situation, just like we had so many times before. "Hello, my name is Philip Cameron, and this is my wife, Chrissie. We've just adopted this boy from Romania."

The brutal response crushed my hope that we had come to the right place. "What have you done to this boy? You have ruined his life. You have made him a nobody; he has no country now. There is nothing we can do!" the man shouted at me.

I would not be moved by his words. God sent me to this place, and there had to be a reason.

Raising my voice, I demanded to see someone in charge. "You do not know what this boy has been through, the hell he has lived in his entire life—starved, abandoned, neglected to the point of child abuse. I want to speak with your supervisor now. My son will come home with me to America."

As soon as the words spilled out, I shut up and let God do the rest. I didn't know what else to do. I was at a dead end, completely out of ideas. Then, from behind, a tall young man stepped forward. With his short, cropped hair and formal manner, he looked to be in the military, but his voice was kind.

"You know what? There might be a way," he said. My heart stopped. I think Chrissie's did as well.

He continued, "There is a provision in American immigration law. It's called *humanitarian parole*, and it states that if we feel that somebody has suffered enough, we waive all the regulations and give the person humanitarian parole. We call it the Mercy Clause."

And that is exactly what they did.

Now he was ours, really ours. We were on our way back to our house.

We'd come to Romania to spend a week; we'd stayed for more than a month. We put everything we owned on the line, in faith, believing that what God said to my heart was true, that this was our little boy.

Several days later, after miles of red tape, we finally heard the roar of a jet plane beneath us. Chrissie was tired but glowing like the new mother she was. She had dressed Andrew in little green corduroys for the trip home to meet his new family.

Everything on the plane fascinated him. He figured out early on in the flight that if he stood on the armrest between us, he could reach the bright orange buttons above.

His motor skills were not as developed as a four-year-old boy's should be; he had been "caged" for too long. But still he scrambled to see all, touch all.

Two switches controlled the lights. Off. On. Off. On. The light switches were great fun, but the best was the red button. It summoned the flight attendant—not that Andrew cared—who would come, roll her eyes, turn off the button, and return to the galley. But he loved the alarm it sounded. Though we tried to interest him in other things every hour he was awake, it was a lost cause.

When we landed at the Atlanta airport eight hours later, Andrew's eyes were as wide as saucers as he took in his surroundings. The sights and the sounds enthralled him. Elevators, escalators, ice cream, telephones ringing, pagers beeping, hamburgers, little golf carts zipping back and forth. For a child who had spent four years in a rusty metal crib, there was so much to take in!

When we pulled into our driveway in Montgomery, Alabama, that November day, a sign, decorated in bright primary colors, fluttered against the front of the house declaring, "Welcome Home, Andrew!" It was one of the happiest sights of my life.

Inside, my dad awaited our arrival. He had come over from Scotland to help with the ministry while we were away and refused to leave until his new grandson arrived.

I sat down on the sofa, put Andrew on my lap, and invited his new siblings and grandfather to get to know him. They tickled him, showed him toys, did everything they could to make him laugh.

Philip Jr. and Melody both had their own bedrooms, and we planned to convert the small study into Andrew's room.

"No way!" eleven-year-old Philip Jr. said when he heard our plan. "My new brother is staying in my room with me!"

Over his shoulder, I caught Chrissie's eye and winked. It was good to be home. It was good to have my boy where he belonged—almost too good to be true.

Hours later, with everyone in bed, I sat watching the last of the embers glow in the fireplace. Silently, I thanked the Lord, praising Him for His goodness, for His mercy for all of us, and especially for my Andrew. I shuddered thinking about where he had come from—the smells, the neglect, the lack of food and water.

"The others are still there."

Where did that thought come from? My mind was racing back and forth. Andrew was here, safe.

The other little faces still in those "cages" flashed before my eyes. Andrew was rescued. The others were not. How would I ever be able to look at Andrew and not think of those other orphans?

Then, I realized that was exactly what God had in mind.

Chapter 11
TV Meets Orphan

Andrew. My son.

Having him in our home after so many months was such a treat. He greeted me each morning with those blue eyes, wide as saucers, filled with delight.

His progress in overcoming his developmental delays was slow but steady. Every struggle he had in holding an object, putting together blocks, or even just walking was a reminder of what he had been through. Watching him took me back to Romania, to the rusty metal cribs, the rows and rows of neglected toddlers.

With Andrew as my daily reminder, it wasn't long before I climbed on another plane back to Romania, determined to do more to help the little ones we'd left behind at his orphanage.

Every few months for seven years, I traveled back there and fixed roofs, painted walls, replaced cribs, and brought food, diapers, formula, and medicine. Chrissie came with me as often as she could, but with a house full of little ones, it was difficult.

On one of my first trips back, just as I was about to take off from the London airport, I called Chrissie one last time. I wanted to check in again before being incommunicado for a while.

I had just gotten her on the phone when she barked, "I'll talk to you later," in a huff.

My sweet wife never talks like that, and I knew better than to let it drop.

"You will tell me now," I said softly. Silence. Then another huff.

"I don't know whether to kill you or congratulate you. I am pregnant!"

I almost dropped the phone. "You are pregnant?" I asked, pretending I hadn't heard her correctly.

"Pregnant."

I repeated the words back into the phone.

"You are pregnant?"

I tried to make peace with Chrissie before hanging up, but I didn't get too far. I found zero humor in the situation. It seemed that overnight we would go from two children to four. After all, we had just adopted Andrew six months before. Who says God doesn't have a sense of humor?

But when sweet Lauren entered the world six months later, there was no doubt that she was God's plan. While she stole my heart as only one's baby girl can do, she also provided unexpected help for Andrew. From the moment we brought her home, Andrew was smitten with her. As she grew, he began to imitate her, developing alongside her and overcoming the last of his delays. It was a plan that only God in His wisdom could have designed.

Chrissie was really stuck at home now while I continued to divide my time between Alabama and Romania.

Overseas, I worked sixteen-hour days, cramming as much work as possible into each trip to Romania so I could be home as often as possible.

I made a point to call on Dana on my first trip back to Romania after bringing Andrew to Alabama. I found her living in an apartment that was totally empty, with not a stick of furniture, not even a bite of food. All she had was a nasty-looking mattress on the floor of the one room and a tiny white hamster in a cage in the corner. Dana was shocked to see me, even though I had promised to stay in touch. I brought with me a small video player and showed her clips of Andrew's progress and growth. Dana's face lit up as she watched her boy chasing a dog across the tiny screen, playing with his brother and sister. Most of all, she couldn't get over his face, how round it was, how healthy, how happy he looked.

At the orphanage, we started with the most basic needs—food, new beds, a working heating system. I hired contractors, marshaled volunteers, brought people and resources from Scotland. Slowly, the place began to show signs of real life. The children at the orphanage grew healthier; the workers came to care more. It was expensive, but worth every dime.

Between trips I traveled from church to church, from telethon to telethon across the United States. It was the ministry's only real source of income to pay for the work with the orphans.

I would tell Andrew's story, detailing the suffering of countless babies who were still stuck in those cribs, and ask God's people to help me.

One invitation brought me to a telethon in the Midwest. I was one of several speakers lined up to help raise the necessary funds for the station—the only Christian television station in the area—to broadcast the gospel, long before cable television.

In the green room, I sat down with a cup of tea and soon was joined by one of the other guests. The man was well-known in Christian circles at the time, bright, charismatic, and engaging to listen to, and he had an impressive track record for raising funds.

He asked about my work, and I casually began telling him the story. We talked for more than an hour, and the more I shared, the more passionate I became. The man sat at the edge of his seat, tearing up as I told stories of the children I met, the conditions in which they lived. I paused as my mind brought me back from all that we had seen to the most immediate needs I was facing in the next few weeks to renovate the next orphanage.

As I sat in the richly appointed room, my flight was less than a month away, and I was still tens of thousands of dollars short to tackle the next phase. I had no clue how I was going to get that money, but I knew that God was in control.

"When are you going next?" he asked, interrupting my thoughts. I told him the dates.

"I am going with you," he said without hesitation. "We will make this happen!"

He was quickly on the phone with his executive secretary, putting together a team of videographers, photographers, and various other workers right before my eyes! I was blown away to think that a professional team finally would see what I saw and be able to tell the tale. The concept had never occurred to me before! I was too busy spending every dime on roofing materials and contractors that it had never occurred to me to spend money on marketing.

Before I knew it, I was in Romania with him and his crew. We were up at sunrise the first morning and on our way to the next orphanage we planned to help. Everything about this place was as bad as that from which Andrew had been rescued. I cautioned my guest and his crew about what to expect, knowing full well my words could not begin to express the horror they were about to see. The people nodded their heads solemnly. "We'll be okay," they seemed to say with their expressions.

We unloaded the truck, and the team got in position. Video cameras in those days weighed about thirty pounds, lighting had to be a higher quality, and on-air talent had to speak into a handheld microphone to be heard.

As soon as all systems were optimized, the crew started toward the building, with cameras rolling.

"I am standing here outside an orphanage in Romania, a small country in Eastern Europe that was once part of the Communist regime," the man spoke into the microphone. "For many years, no one knew what was happening behind the borders of this country. Her people are poor, the jobless rate is over 50 percent, and bread and meat are scarce even if you have money to pay for them. This is a country where they throw away their babies."

He artfully stopped speaking and let the grave words sink in. "Parents abandon their babies like yesterday's newspaper. They are thrown away in a trash heap or at a neighbor's house, or left in the hospital beds they were born in. What happens to these babies . . . hundreds of thousands of innocent children? Let me show you."

He dropped his microphone from his face, and the videographer signaled, "Cut."

Wow, I thought, that was powerful.

I could see the value in using good media to tell the story and was excited to see how this turned out.

The team gathered its equipment and started for the building door. The talent got the signal to begin, and he looked into the camera one last time with the door closed behind him. Pausing for effect, he closed his eyes for a second, and then he threw open the heavy metal door, letting out an audible gasp as he did so.

As he walked in, still facing the camera, his eyes filled with tears as the smell of urine overwhelmed him. The crew coughed into their elbows to muffle the sounds from the video. With the cameras rolling, the man started to speak, though I had to strain to hear his words.

His voice trembling with emotion, the man began going from crib to crib.

"There must be a hundred babies in this room, and there is not an adult in sight. This little girl, poor thing, look at her. Someone chopped off all her hair. Why is she naked? Can't someone at least put a diaper on this child? She is so thin I can see her ribs," he called over his shoulder.

"Look, she is trying to grab my finger, but she is too weak. And this little boy. What is wrong with him? Look at those bruises. He could not have done this himself, could he? Dear Lord. And this one."

Crib to crib, room to room, the video continued. I watched for a while, but I needed to get some other work done. Forcing myself to focus, I sat off in the corner with a notebook as he taped, jotting down the items I needed to purchase in town that night: light bulbs, skin cream, sixteen windowpanes to replace those that were broken.

His next segment interrupted my thoughts: "I need your help. It will cost two hundred thousand dollars to make this place livable for these children. Just one hundred dollars will pay for a new crib with a soft mattress, a warm blanket, and real sheets. Just three hundred dollars will replace a single window—and we have twenty that must be replaced before the bitter winter descends on these babies. It will cost fifty thousand dollars just to fix the roof."

Brilliant, I thought. No wonder he is a "star" in Christian circles, and I am just the guy buying the light bulbs.

From there we went across town to the home where I had found my Andrew. It was the first home we helped, and it was so different that I hardly recognized it. The floors were new and sparkling clean, and there were new cribs, new linens, and bright toys with which the children could play. The children were well-fed and diapered, and a row of plastic potty seats lined the wall under the new windows. The television crew members were tired when they arrived but jumped with life at what they saw. Now this was a story!

I beamed with pride as they documented the great work that had been done. The talent took one well-dressed child after the other in his arms, his moving commentary flowing with no script or cue cards. "It is amazing what a few dollars from generous people can do. Look at these new windows. These children have nothing to fear this winter. The roof over their heads is new." On and on he went about all the great things God's people had done.

Soon, the light of the day began to fade. I was out of energy myself, and I would sleep well that night knowing that the need was well documented, that others would share my burden for these kids.

The next day, I saw the crew off to the airport. We hugged and shook hands, and I was told to expect to hear from them shortly.

I returned to my work on both sides of the ocean. Days turned into weeks, weeks to months. Finally, I was back in Montgomery, enjoying a simple night of family time and television.

As I surfed from one channel to the next, the man's face suddenly filled my nineteen-inch screen. Behind him was the Romanian orphanage. I leaned forward in my easy chair and turned up the sound. I listened first with interest, then with horror. The man was on the air taking credit for all the work we had done and asking for money to do more. His 800 number and address were on the screen. The closing announcer said there was no time to lose.

It was the closest I came to hearing from the man or his crew again, and I certainly never saw a penny of that money. I can't say if the children of Romania did either.

I was tempted to call him, hire a lawyer, and threaten him, but the Lord would not let me. Sure, I nursed resentment, but anytime I dwelled on it for too long, the Lord would convict me that this was His work, not mine. The man had taken advantage of His orphans, not mine.

My job was not to call this man out; my job was to keep doing what God called me to do. So I threw myself even deeper into my work.

The next trip I had planned was for the first week of December. As I was preparing for my visit, Chrissie was just starting to deck the halls for our family Christmas.

Romania was steeped in the traditions of the Orthodox Church, and Christmas is celebrated on January 7 there.

The thought excited me and quickly turned into a plan. I would get to take Christmas to orphans who had never had gifts in their lives. What a treat that would be! Chrissie, the kids, the staff, and every friend I had flew into action. Dolls, toy trucks, bouncy balls, pretty ribbons, candies, and more were packed into boxes and loaded into my van.

That year was the first of what has become a tradition, evolving into tens of thousands of shoe box-sized plastic bins that we hand deliver to children back at the orphanage we first transformed—Andrew's "home." Soon, the Christmas boxes became the icing on the cake in our work with orphans. As we focused on one home after the other, we got to know the children.

By returning annually to each home after all the reconstruction had been finished, we could make sure everything was being properly managed and check on the children. Plus, it was great fun.

Throughout the next seven years, we worked in Romania, improving conditions and the lives of countless children. By then, either our ministry or another had targeted every orphanage we could find in the country, and conditions drastically improved for the orphans of Romania.

In December of 1996, I arrived in Budapest, Hungary, to meet the team who had brought the Christmas boxes from Scotland to hand out in Romania. Days before I was scheduled to leave, the phone rang. It was my dad. "I've just read in the British press about another country in desperate need." It began to sound like a *Groundhog's Day* sequel. "The story I've read was about freezing children. Don't stay with the team from Scotland in Romania. I want you to go to Moldova and see if the things I've read are true."

Moldova? I had never heard of Moldova, much less thought of visiting there.

"Where is Moldova?" I asked.

"It's just one country over," my dad replied. "Just keep driving when you get to Romania."

To make sure I understood that he meant business, he told me the title of a newspaper article on Moldova's orphanages. The headline read, "The Dying Rooms of Moldova." Though it was hard for me to comprehend what he was saying, Dad described conditions far worse than any I had seen, even in Romania.

I read up about Moldova and learned that this tiny country, about the size of Maryland, was once part of Romania, who joined with the Germans against Russia. When defeated, Russia annexed Moldova into the Soviet Union. Moldova became independent in 1991 when the Soviet Union fell apart.

When the Iron Curtain fell, many thought it would again become part of Romania; after all, they shared the same language and much of the same history and culture, but the leaders decided to become an independent nation. It quickly became the poorest nation in all of Europe.

The level of poverty in this small nation is beyond the comprehension of most Americans. We have no problem visualizing the poor in Africa, in Haiti. We have seen enough videos and photos to picture the small stick huts with dirt floors and no water or electricity.

But this is Europe! How can this nation have the majority of her people living in mud houses, without electricity, using bathrooms that are just holes in the ground behind the house? But that is the reality, and to make matters worse, in winter the temperature drops as low as twenty below zero.

Through research, I learned that this was a Third World country by any standard. And my dad was sending me there as casually as you would send someone to the corner store for a gallon of milk.

On the trip, the snow was shoulder high, and the journey took me across the Carpathian Mountains on the narrowest, most dangerous road I had ever traveled.

The only thing I can compare these mountains to are the cartoon mountains in *How the Grinch Stole Christmas!* They seemed to go straight up into the sky, and the tiny road wound up and down them with no guardrails at all. The snow was piled up on the sides so high that it was hard to tell where the road ended and the snowbank began. There were no streetlights, and there was very little traffic. I had fleeting thoughts that if we were to go over the edge and down into the snow, no one would find us until the spring thaw.

But onward I drove. We spoke little, but I had found it to be normal. My translator wasn't a great one. But he understood more than he spoke. It was enough to get by. His English, to put it kindly, was rudimentary at best. We communicated in the simplest of forms. "Food?" "Da" (Yes), and he'd point to where I should stop to eat. "Gas?" "Da." He'd jump out to fill the tank. Finally, we made it to the border of Moldova. I had a map of the country and the location of one of the orphanages. It was in a village called Hincesti.

We arrived around noon at the doorway of the building that would change my life forever. It was another typical building "designed" by the Communists, box-like and painted an ugly shade of tan.

The bitterly cold wind lashed my face as I opened the door and stepped out onto the driveway. Looking more carefully at the building, I saw that many of the windows were broken; some were missing entirely with nothing left but rotten frames. I shook my head in disgust. It looked like it had been decades since anything was painted or repaired. Garbage littered the walkway, and the smell made me nauseated. Around the walls about eighteen inches or so away were piles of human waste. With no toilets working they squatted against the wall to relieve themselves.

Discarded clothes, shoes, papers, and broken toys were all piled up in random heaps in the snow.

I walked through the door and braced myself for what I would find. It didn't help. The familiar smells of urine, filth, body odor, and garbage overwhelmed me. I pressed on, hating every moment, but knowing full well that this was an appointment the Lord had ordained.

As I walked in, I shook the snow off my shoes. The director, Mr. Ciubotari, met me at the foyer. A short man with a red face and dark eyes, he shook my hand and welcomed me without even a hint of shame at the conditions of the place. I looked past him and saw dirty blankets nailed over the broken windows in a feeble attempt to keep out the cold.

The children in this home were all handicapped, and they huddled together in the middle of one large room. Each was wearing layers of mismatched and ill-fitting clothing. It looked as though they had been handed a pile of clothing with no regard to its condition or size, and they were wearing every single bit of it just to stay alive.

The room was frighteningly quiet. Even though there were several children in front of me, no one said a word, made eye contact, or acknowledged I was there at all. Each child stared off into space, a few rocking and a few asleep in their chairs. It was the most hopeless collection of children I had ever seen in my life.

The director broke the silence. "Have you ever seen a baby freeze to death?"

I stopped and turned. "What did you say?"

"Have you ever seen a baby freeze to death?" he repeated.

Chapter 12
Hincesti Orphanage, Freezing Babies

"Have you ever seen a baby freeze to death?"

The words hung in the frozen air. Had I ever seen a baby freeze to death?

I looked at him, stunned.

He continued, "Already sixteen children have frozen to death this winter."

It was only December 11.

The thought of these helpless children was more than I could deal with, and I couldn't get the words or the image out of my mind as I toured the building. First, he showed me the equipment used to heat the facility. Of the three coal-fired boilers, only one worked, and it didn't work well. In fact, it looked to be about a hundred years old.

It required coal, of course, but the coal bunker was empty. The tiny flame that danced inside was quickly disappearing as it devoured the few twigs and branches someone had tossed inside.

"Thirty children froze to death here last year," he added offhandedly. "All of them died in their beds."

Touching the metal beds in the subzero weather was like touching a flagpole outside during a winter storm. If I were to touch my tongue to the bedpost, it would instantly freeze. I couldn't imagine a worse way to die than with raw skin affixed to frozen metal.

Every room of the dreadful place was freezing, every child was listless, and his or her eyes were vacant. The only movement I saw was when lunch was placed in front of the children. Each child grabbed the plate and ate the tiny bit of gruel as quickly as possible. I could not recognize anything on the plate other than a few grains of rice, but they lapped the spilled rice from the tables like hungry dogs.

I struggled to make sense of it all. I was less than a day's drive from some of the world's most powerful economies, and children—even babies—were freezing to death in their beds, starving, without any hope at all! I walked around following the director. My hands thrust deeply in my pockets. I screamed inside my head in a desperate attempt to separate reality from my mind and heart. "This is a movie. It's not real."

To make matters worse—if that was even possible—these children were not only orphans; they were also disabled. Some were blind. Many were in wheelchairs. Some were mentally disabled. What a cruel life! I had to escape this place. I began to make excuses to go. It was not to be. The director interrupted my thoughts. "The children would like to sing for you." I was stuck. I couldn't refuse. They sang a couple of Romanian songs. The old accordion wheezed as it was played. I kept thinking I wish they would stop and let me go. "Tell them I love them." It was His voice speaking to me to do the absurd. "Tell them You love them?" I thought in my mind that I didn't want to embarrass God by telling these tragic waifs that God loved them. These pitiful souls had woken up in the morning with their friends lying beside them frozen to death. "Love them?" You must be kidding. He spoke again. "Tell them." I moved to the accordionist and motioned for him to pump the bellows. I sang in what must have been the worst translation of "Jesus Loves Me." As I sang, I was embarrassed. I was mad. How could I be singing "Jesus Loves Me" to these forgotten dying kids? My song was finished. I'd done it. I told them God loved them. Now all I could think about was getting out of this hellhole and into my van and putting as many miles as I could between me, them, Moldova, EVERYTHING. This just wasn't fair. I paused and took away my hand from the accordion keyboard and began to turn and head for the door. As I did God sprung the trap and took the moment and my life out of my hands. They started to sing a song, and I recognized the tune. The words in English are:

> This is the day, this is the day
> That the Lord hath made, that the Lord hath made
> I will rejoice, I will rejoice
> And be glad in it, and be glad in it

My heart melted at the familiar tune. I could no longer keep an emotional distance from these children, even if I wanted to. God had brought me into their lives to change them, to show them His love. I could no longer simply curse the Communists, the bureaucracy, their parents, the director, or staff; I had to do something.

If these children stayed in these conditions, if another one froze to death, it would be my fault. I had seen this, experienced this, and knew firsthand how bad it was. These were not children in a book or magazine; they were in front of me, singing their hearts out, so cold that their lips were blue.

No one would freeze to death in this building again, not as long as I had breath in my body. After a while I found myself sitting in the director's office. I could see my breath as I talked. The director explained that during the worst night of the year, he had moved all of the children into a single room so they could stay as warm as possible. By daylight, seven of those children were dead.

As soon as I heard that, I started making a plan. Could I get coal with my credit cards? No. Could we board up the broken windows until I could buy new ones? We had to move, and we had to move quickly. I did a quick calculation as to how much cash I needed to get back to Hungary where my credit cards would work. The director suggested that if we could find a man in the village who could patch up the windows with smaller holes, he would make a patch with glass and glue it in place. Within minutes a call was made, and he was on his way. Whatever money was left I gave to Mr. Ciubotari to buy food and made a mad dash back across Europe to the airplane. I had to find the money for coal.

I was in the airport waiting for my plane when I saw a friend, Rusty Nelson, waiting for the same flight to Atlanta. He sat beside me and asked how things were. It was his first mistake. I wept and tried to explain to him the unexplainable. He wept with me. I gave him a video that I had taken. "Rusty," I said, "up until this moment this was my responsibility alone, and now it's yours as well." We hugged. He took that tape, showed it in the church where he was the worship leader at New Life in Jacksonville, Florida. They received an offering. A miracle was on its way. I flew to Columbus, Ohio, to be with my dear friends Sam and Paulette Farina at Christian Assembly. They opened their hearts and wallets. I had enough money to buy the coal. In a matter of days, I was back on a plane on my way to Moldova.

Days later, there was a roaring fire in the furnace. The children were no longer in danger, and as long as I could supply eighteen hundred dollars a month for coal, they never would be again.

Like I had done in the Romanian orphanages, I started working alongside a team to transform this state-run orphanage into a real home. Once the most basic needs—heat, windows, and food—were met, we were able to bring Christmas gifts.

The kids began to recognize our truck as soon as it was in sight. I'd open the door to the sounds of delighted children calling my name, "Feeleep! Feeleep!" Over time, our work was matched by work from other nonprofits in Europe. The building was completely remodeled, and the children had the best living conditions they'd ever known. I was so pleased to see the positive change.

It was time to move on to the next chapter in my life and ministry.

Chapter 13
What's That Blue Sign?

It was a wonderful feeling knowing that the "heavy lifting" part of my work in Moldova was over. A corporation in Europe finally adopted the orphanage in Hincesti and rebuilt it from top to bottom. I could rest easy knowing that the children would always have heat and a solid roof over their heads.

I planned a "fun trip."

This was a new concept to me, to go visit the orphans in Moldova and just bring Christmas gifts. I felt like Santa himself. Someone else was now providing the heat, and I would feel the joy of being able to put all my efforts into bringing Christmas cheer to the children.

I was able to bring Melody and Andrew along with me. It would be a great treat for them—and for the orphans—to play together, to discover each of the toys in the boxes and to learn how to play with them. Traveling over, I was in a great mood.

The trip itself was uneventful. We flew to Munich, Germany, with Tom Valley, a doctor from Columbus, Ohio. He was a new friend and supporter, a tall man with a bald head and gold wire-trim glasses. A likable character with an easy smile. His personality made the time pass quickly. We rented a passenger van and drove to Moldova to meet up with our truck from Scotland. When we arrived there, Willie Moffatt, a rather crusty truck driver that was part of Dad's ministry in Scotland, had the truck filled with boxes of toys. He had driven the 2,500 miles from Romania.

I was anxious to see everybody and have a big old-fashioned holiday with my kids and the orphans. We had hot chocolate, candy canes, and lots of special treats that would be new for the kids. It was amazing!

As we started down the road away from the orphanage, I let my mind wander. I would now have more time with my family, more time to preach, more time to study. Life would continue at a much calmer pace.

Heavy snow began falling, but it seemed fitting. It was Christmas, after all, and the van was warm. There was only one final stop to make, a few more gifts to deliver in an orphanage of five hundred kids in the town of Leova.

As the weather got worse, though, I wondered how many hours the weather conditions would add to the trip. Traveling with my kids, there was always the constant chorus of, "When will we get there? Are we there yet?" from the back seat. Other than that, the only noise we heard was caused by the van hitting the frequent potholes.

The sky was gray and dim; it was as though the world outside the van was a black-and-white photograph. The snow was deep and piled high on either side of the road, and the landscape offered only bare, dark trees swaying in the winter wind. On the way to Leova, Dr. Tom nudged me with his elbow. He pointed to a blue sign on the side of the road that said "Orfani." He pointed and said, "Look! There is another orphanage." I didn't reply. I wanted to get the gifts in the back of Willie's truck delivered; then it was back home.

On the way back from Leova, Dr. Tom began to nag about the sign again. "Let's go and see this place."

"No, Tom, the snow is getting worse. We need to be on our way back."

He wouldn't stop. "You never know what is down that road." As he went on, I grew more annoyed. I knew what would happen. He would be back home in a few days, continuing his work at his successful practice, and I would be stuck down that snow-packed road.

I glanced at the large blue-and-white sign that said "Casa de Copii Orfani - 3km"—House for the Orphan Children. An arrow pointed to a tiny road, barely visible in the snow.

"Oh no," I said, shaking my head. "I am not going there." I knew better than to look and see. No way was he talking me into this.

"We are here, Philip. Come on, let's take a look."

I would not be persuaded. It was time for a bit of logic.

"Look at the snow; are you kidding me? We'll get the van stuck in the snow, and we'll be walking back to Germany."

Finally, he wore me down enough to go along with it. I figured we would get out, decide the road was too narrow, and keep moving. I signaled for Willie to pull over and waited for him to walk over to us. All three of us looked down the road where the sign pointed.

"Willie, tell the man. We can't get up that road can't we?" It was as negative a statement as I could make. "This is crazy," I retorted.

Willie interrupted in his thick Scottish accent, "Aye, aye. I think we can do this. You go first in the van, and if you get stuck I'll pull you out with my chain. Let's give it a go." I looked at Willie; he had just taken away my last excuse. "Thanks, pal. Thanks"

Then Andrew piped up. "Come on, Dad, let's go see. What's the harm?"

"I need to stretch my legs anyway, so let's go see what's up there," Melody added.

There was no point in trying to fight them all.

So up the long road we went. As soon as we entered the village of Cupcui, we saw a large building, again with all the hallmarks of a Communist designed institution. The ugly, drab building with a flat roof looked like a giant box with little square windows sitting in the snow.

It was almost dark, but there was a faint light coming from a few of the windows. For a moment, I thought the building might be abandoned. We parked anyway and started up the broken steps.

As I walked through the front door, I was overwhelmed with the familiar toxic smells of filth, urine, garbage, and poor hygiene.

Here we go again, I thought, suddenly feeling very tired. Then in the gloom I saw a man standing. I learned later that he was the director of the orphanage.

The place was as bad as, if not worse than, anyplace I had ever seen. Black mold covered the walls, and there was no light at all in the foyer. Down the hall I heard singing.

Curious, we walked toward the source of the music and soon entered a large room with more than one hundred children huddled together in two groups. One group was on the left side of the room, and the other group was on the right.

It was the strangest thing. They were giving a concert, but there was no audience. No mothers or fathers or friends. In fact, the one adult in the room wore an expression of either sheer boredom or outright disgust. She was obviously only there because she was paid to be; it was nothing more than a job.

In all of my life, I had never seen anything sadder. These children were celebrating Christmas the only way they knew how, by taking turns singing to one another in this dark, dingy room. Not a single parent was there to cheer them on; all they had was one another and their songs.

Immediately, the children went silent as they noticed us walk in. I am sure we scared them at first, as they did not know what to expect from us. The room was freezing cold. Some of the children didn't even have coats.

"No, please, sing, sing!" I motioned with my hands.

Andrew and Melody followed my lead and began to clap and repeat: "Sing! Sing!"

Looking at one another in surprise, the children began singing again, this time a bit louder, happier. After each song, we clapped like crazy, encouraging them, trying to show how delighted we were with the music. We didn't understand a word they were singing, but we were determined to be the best audience we could be.

As I smiled and listened, my mind was racing. All the Christmas boxes were gone. I had no more toys, no more candy, nothing left to give these kids. My heart sank at the thought. I leaned over to Melody; "These kids are singing for us and we have absolutely nothing to give them." I couldn't enjoy their songs for this nagging thought.

Then, out of nowhere, I heard the words, "Don't just bring them things. Be their dad."

I looked from face to face, child to child. These kids were beautiful, sad, hopeless, and forgotten.

"Be their dad."

How could I possibly do that? Repairing roofs and windows was one thing, but being a dad is a whole different kettle of fish.

After the singing, I set about getting to know as many of the children as I could in the short time we were there. One of the first kids I reached out to was a pale girl who looked to be about fourteen. Her hair was a soft brown, and she had a cute upturned nose, like a button. I later learned her name was Galina.

She was one of the shyest children in the room, hanging back in the corner. I had to draw her out to get her to interact with me. She was a sad, broken little thing.

During my next visits, it seemed she always had a cleaning rag in her hand; she was trying to busy herself, I guess. The others would push her toward me, and she would duck away. As I got to know her, it was plain to see that there was something terribly, terribly wrong with her. She squinted all the time. She struggled to see. Every now and then, she would make a face, like a flash of pain had hit her in the head.

Galina was the youngest of three children. When her parents divorced, Galina was only three. Her mother took her other two children, and for reasons Galina will never know, she was left behind.

Galina, this tiny slip of a girl, was dropped off in an orphanage for preschoolers with more than two hundred other little ones. Like the others in that part of Moldova, she spoke only Russian.

The home was short-staffed, and the staff, short-tempered. Galina quickly learned to be the invisible one in a sea of toddlers. She was hungry and cold, but her heart was fixed on one thing—seeing her parents again. But they never came, never wrote, and never called . . . ever.

Meanwhile, adults regularly visited the orphanage in search of little ones to adopt. Galina was one of the few whose parents never signed over parental rights.

Because of that, she could never be adopted. One by one, her friends were adopted, and once again, she was left wondering why she was the only one left alone.

So not only did she feel the pain of abandonment, but also she had no hope of escaping the orphanage and being part of a real family.

Every day for this little girl was a nightmare of shouting, threats, and relentless beatings. Somehow, she learned to read and write enough to be ready for school in September, but that started another sad chapter of her life.

In Moldova, the worst thing you can be is an orphan. Orphans are hated, despised, treated like they are less than humans. But they are still sent to attend public school with the village children, who often call the orphans names and make up nasty songs about them. Teachers look the other way, and the director of the orphanage doesn't care.

The rules were harsh for a little girl as scared as Galina. If she was late getting back to the orphanage and lunch was over, she'd have nothing to eat until supper. The workers would taunt her, making sure she knew they were taking her food home to feed their cows and pigs. At Cupcui Orphanage, the conditions were horrendous. The roof leaked, and her bed was often wet at night. She and the other girls would try to push the beds around to find a dry spot, but it was a useless endeavor.

It was also cold. The windows were broken, the heat didn't work, and little Galina stood beside me with no coat, just a few layers of dirty sweaters.

And God told me to be Galina's dad.

Years later, she told me that the day I met her, she was so sad it felt like she had a "black heart." She wondered, as she had wondered every Christmas, how come even Santa Claus hated orphans. Why did he bring presents to everyone but orphans?

She also had been thinking about her mother a lot. As she was singing in that cold little room with the other orphans, she imagined that her mother was in the audience clapping, beaming with pride at her performance.

And it was in the midst of that longing that we showed up.

Before we left that day, I wanted to give them something, anything. All I could do was cheer them on as they sang. Finally, Melody remembered that she had some little stickers in the truck, and rushed out to get them.

Years later, Galina shared how much that silly little sticker meant to her. "I kept it on my face for days, just touching it and remembering that someone smiled at me and gave this to me. I didn't understand why they came, why they seemed to like us, since we were nothing but orphans. But it was a wonderful Christmas present."

I was stunned to feel so deeply about these children so quickly. I felt like they were mine.

The last thing I did before I left that day was tour the facility so I could see the whole place. I began to make a list of what structural things needed to be accomplished to make this orphanage livable.

There was not a warm spot in the whole building. The showers were outside in another unheated building with nothing but a steady drip of cold water coming from the faucet. In the warmer months, five girls at a time were allowed a five-minute shower. In the dead of winter, they didn't bother; it was just too cold. The toilets were a small squat building outside and to the left. I went there and even though it was bitterly cold, the stench of human waste caught my breath. Tears rolled down my cheeks. My own daughter Melody, and my adopted son, Andrew, were inside playing with kids whose lives were completely different than anything they knew. If Melody had to use these vile toilets or shower in that filthy stall a hundred yards from the orphanage, I couldn't even bear the thought. I was beginning to understand just how evil this communist system was to those that Jesus described as "the least of these."

In Moldova, the government closes the orphanages in the summer and sends the children back to their families for "vacation" or to other families that are each paid eleven cents per day to keep the children. Most of these children who are placed in families for pay are put to work on the farms, tending sheep, weeding gardens, and at night, often suffer at the hands of abusive, drunken adults. It's no vacation. But for me, their "vacation" would give me three months to turn this place into something more habitable before they returned.

It took a long time and a lot of money. We replastered and painted the walls cheerful colors and divided the large ward-like rooms into smaller, homier bedrooms. And then I sent the water out for testing.

"Faulty test" was the message I got back. So, more carefully, we took the test again.

"Faulty test" was the second message. The third test revealed the same results. Finally, a scientist from the lab came and took the sample himself.

Two days later, I had the results. They had never seen water so filthy. The water in that well was contaminated with sewer from the apartment building just above the orphanage. My stomach turned. These children I loved had been drinking sewer water for years.

That finding set us back until we could raise the money to dig new, deeper, safer wells.

I looked at Galina and the other children, and I silently made them a promise: I'd be back. I'd be back, and I'd make sure those wells were dug. I'd be back, and I would make this place more like a home. They would see how much I loved and valued them as children, and then it would be easier for them to understand that Jesus loves them, too.

One day I visited the village school. As I walked through the corridors and looked into the classrooms, I came to where Galina was studying. Something was wrong. She was older than all the other kids in the class. I asked a simple question. "Why?" The answer I received was astounding. Galina couldn't see the blackboard. Year after year she had been held back by teachers that didn't care or bother about the young girl squinting at the board. Their explanation as they hissed their hate towards this orphan: "You are stupid. You didn't pass your test again. You must repeat the year." That day I took her to the capital to an optometrist.

Her equipment was ancient, but her diagnosis was clear. Galina was almost blind. She put some glasses on Galina close to what she needed, and the young girl who had lived for years in a fog of blindness, gasped. All she needed was a pair of glasses.

Chapter 14
Can We Call You Mom and Dad?

"Be their dad." The words rattled around in my brain as I tried to process what that meant on the way home.

Right away, I got to work raising the money and gathering the supplies needed to transform the orphanage over the summer. But I needed to do more than that; I also had two hundred new children for whom to provide.

There was Tania, a petite little thing who made everyone around her laugh. She mimicked a thousand voices and had the perfect comic timing of a clown.

Of all the children, she was the only one I could really talk to from the first day. She had taught herself an amazing amount of English from the little bit of television the orphans were allowed to watch. (Most of the time, the workers had it on the news.)

When I asked about her past, though, her smiling face turned dark. "There is a memory I have that never leaves me," she said. "It is there all the time. I was very little and was sleeping when I heard my father's angry voice. He was drunk and locked outside the house. He was pounding on the door with his fist, demanding that my mother come outside."

Finally, Tania's mother opened the door and went outside to her husband. Scared for her mother,

Tania went to the window and saw that she was on the ground, her father beating her brutally.

"He kicked and kicked her until she stopped moving," she told me. "I ran out the back door and went to my neighbor's house. I begged them to come and stop my father from hurting my mother." But the help was too late. Tania's mother was left handicapped for life from that beating. That one event resulted in Tania and her sisters being taken to the orphanage and her mom's giving in to the temptation of alcohol as a means of escaping the pain.

"I remember being so scared when she left me at the orphanage. I ran after my mother, but they grabbed me and brought me back. I wanted my mother, but no one cared."

Blinking back a tear, Tania continued, "When I dream, it is always of my mother. Then I wake up and find myself still in the orphanage. Sometimes I still wonder how I can face another day without my mother."

Every child had a story that was worse than the last. With each one I heard, it was as if God was saying, "Philip, you think this place is bad, that living here is the worst thing that could happen to a child? Don't kid yourself. Their homes, their parents were far worse. The orphanage is better, but you know they need more. They need a dad, and you are it." I knew what I had to do. From a construction point of view, this place was a much larger project than the orphanage in Hincesti— worse even than the orphanages in Romania. It would take hundreds of thousands of dollars and more faith and prayer than I was sure I was capable of.

In less than a year, we replaced every window, installed indoor toilets and showers, added a water filter for the well and built a new roof. We put in new beds, carpets, everything to make it into a real home. Making Chrissie and myself available to these children as their dad and mom was also a much larger project. Parenting required time, one-on-one; dependable, consistent time.

During all the years I had traveled to Romania and early on in Moldova, my work had centered on orphanages near cities large enough that I could stay nearby in a motel. It wasn't by design; it had just worked out that way.

But in Cupcui, I faced two issues. First, it was a three-hour round trip by car to the closest city where there were motels. And second, this calling to be dad and mom to these children meant I needed to be there. With my time divided now among my travels to minister and raise funds, my family in the States, and my work in Moldova, I needed to make as much as I could of each day in Moldova.

Most days, we started out on the trip at first light. But one day, we left the hotel later than usual so that we could swing through downtown. As we turned left to head out of town, we saw something we had never noticed before: the golden arches of McDonald's.

I stopped right in the middle of the intersection, cars honking and people behind me yelling at me in Romanian. I didn't care; I had an idea. Moments later, I stood in front of the shiny counter and spoke to the fresh-faced cashier.

"One hundred hamburgers," I slowly said, making sure they understood what I'd said.

"One hundred?"

Pulling my wallet out of my back pocket, I nodded. I knew the orphans had never heard of McDonald's or even eaten a hamburger.

This would be a great treat, regardless of the fact that the burgers would be stone cold by the time we got to the orphanage.

Two hours later, we entered the orphanage with six bags. At first, the kids weren't even sure what to do with the sandwiches, but they soon figured it out and wolfed them down and licked their fingers after they were finished.

All but one girl. She took her hamburger—wrapper and all—to her room. Hours later, I found her in her room still staring at it. To her, it was too precious to eat.

Shortly after that, Chrissie and I decided that the best thing to do was to buy a small house as close to the orphanage as possible so that we would have somewhere to stay during our visits. Most of the people in the village lived in hovels. Finding a house with flushing toilets, showers, working heat, and electricity was a challenge in itself.

Finally, we settled on a white cottage near the end of a dirt road just ten minutes from the orphanage. There was a well in the garden; we added a pump, bringing running water into the house.

Most of our neighbors were trying to survive by farming and had all manner of ducks and chickens in their yards. Our trip up the gravel road often was slowed behind a wooden wagon filled with produce, pulled by a horse that had seen better days. It was like going back in time. When our little house was finally finished, the neighbor knocked on the door. He spoke Romanian to me, but I understood nothing. To my surprise he pushed his way past me and made a beeline toward the bathroom. He paused for a second and pushed the lever on the side of the toilet. It was the first time for this old man to flush a toilet.

We had forged a relationship with the orphanage director. By the time we were ready to open the home for visits from orphans, he agreed to let us bring eight or ten kids at a time over for the weekend. Galina and Tania were in the first group of eight to be our special guests. Except for the walk to school each day and "vacation" in the summer, these kids never left the orphanage. They had no concept of the outside world.

As we opened the door of our mission house, I tried to see it through their eyes. After entering the small mudroom, the first thing they saw was a closet filled with clean pajamas, socks, and slippers.

"Really? For us? We get to wear those?" they squealed with joy like kids at Christmas.

Chrissie was quick to nod and explain that the first thing we wanted them each to do was take a hot shower and change into these comfy, clean clothes.

Hot showers? One at a time? New clothes to wear? Wide-eyed, they took in every room of the house with raw and pure joy beyond anything I had ever seen. The house was filled with the smells of the dinner Chrissie was making. Good old-fashioned spaghetti and meatballs was on the menu with green salad and fresh bread.

The kids joked with one another as they "fought" over who would shower first. Tania was goofing around in the living room with the other kids, imitating the ducks in the yard, their schoolteacher, and, when she thought I wasn't listening, me.

Galina alone found her way to Chrissie's side, sweeping the floor that was already clean, wiping down the tables, doing anything she could think of to help. The others found jigsaw puzzles in the corner of the living room and began to put it together, giggling as if these were the most amazing things on planet earth.

It was the first of many wonderful nights with the kids, the groups changing each weekend. Sometimes we'd go into the city for a special treat—a trip for pizza or shopping at the market.

One night I wanted to show them the story of Jesus. "I have a movie I want you to watch with me," I told the girls.

The kids were excited to see a movie, no matter the topic.

"Do you know who Jesus is?" I asked, looking up at their blank faces. "He is God, who came to earth as a man."

"Who is God?" one girl asked.

I started to explain but stopped myself. "Let's watch together; then we can talk."

Campus Crusade for Christ and the Jesus Film Project translated this amazing movie, originally produced more than twenty years ago, into countless languages. They took great care, using natives in the countries to recreate the dialogue into the language of people who had little ministry material available to them.

This was and still is an amazing tool to use to introduce Jesus to the orphans that is beyond my personal ability. I had spent hundreds of hours showing them the love of Christ through my actions, but they still didn't understand. In a few moments they would know why we did what we were doing.

As we darkened the lights, the kids flopped down on the couches, piling on top of one another like a litter of kittens. Chrissie had placed out bowls of popcorn, and I was amazed to see that as soon as the movie started, the girls ignored the buttery snack. The story on the television, the greatest story ever told, had their undivided attention. To give them space, Chrissie and I sat behind the laptop screen. We couldn't see the movie; all we saw was the expressions on their beautiful faces.

Years later, Galina told me, "I never really trusted you at first. I had many people come into my life and leave. The more I loved them, the more I hurt, so I decided not to love you and Mom or anyone."

She shared that with me, and though she was glad for the presents I brought and for making the orphanage so much better to live in, she didn't understand why I did it.

"It didn't make sense," she said. "We were nothing but orphans. Why leave your family to come and spend time with us? It was too good to be true, and I knew it would not last, so I kept my distance.

"You never talked about Jesus unless we asked. You would say, 'I love you this much [holding her hands about a foot apart], but Jesus loves you this much [holding her hands out as wide as she could].' But that made no sense to me. Who was Jesus? I never saw Him. If He was God, He certainly didn't care about me. I was an orphan. I didn't deserve anything. My own mother and father left me and never tried to find me. Jesus loved me? No way."

As she watched the Jesus movie, Galina said that God came to earth for her.

"He loved children. When they put Him on the cross, I began to weep and weep. I could not stop crying," she said. "My hard heart was not so hard. I asked Jesus into my heart that night, though I still understood so little."

It was very late when the movie was over, but the girls begged to watch it again. After pressing "play," I quickly fell asleep in my chair. The girls stayed awake to watch every word again. They could not get enough of it.

For the first time, Galina realized, "Jesus loves me! He sees me! He knows my name! He cares when I am hungry, alone, sick, scared. He is there and will never leave me. It was the greatest night of my life to discover this. Then your love became easier for me to understand. I went back to the orphanage after the weekend sad that our time was over and we had to go back to that terrible place, but my heart changed. I had hope."

The Jesus film soon brought up many questions from the children, and their questions became my invitation to tell them story after story from the Word of God.

Seeing Jesus come to life in the movie made my gospel messages to the children easier to grasp and gave them a deep desire to know more about God.

Those weekends were incredible times with the kids. One by one, they let down their guards like Galina did. We all grew closer—like a family. With every hour, I, Dad, grew, too, in my love and care for these incredible children with whom God had entrusted me.

We did everything we could to make the kids we couldn't bring to the mission house feel special, too. Chrissie and the kids would make massive trays of Jell-O—strawberry, lime, pineapple—and then carry them back to the orphanage. The kids had never seen Jell-O before, and their pleasure was intoxicating. I laughed until I hurt, watching them play with the "food."

We grew closer to these children than any with whom we had ever worked. Chrissie and I came to see them as our children in a way that I cannot describe. When we were in America, we could not wait to get back. When we were in Moldova, we could not wait to raise more money and make life easier for "our kids."

I made a point to communicate with these kids without learning Romanian. I knew that if they saw how much I cared, they would want to talk to me, and it would give them a reason to learn English—a life skill that would give them an advantage.

We spent hours and hours with each of them, teaching one word at a time. "Book." "Glasses." "Cookie." "Hair." Then a big one: "Grade." Chrissie played endless hours of the matching game. Each time a card was flipped over, she would say "cow," and they would repeat "cow" or "horse" and they would repeat "horse." They usually would win the game. Their hunger to learn was amazing.

Each of the kids quickly learned to get his or her report card ready for us when we were there. We wanted to have a connection with each of them so that they knew someone cared if they passed or failed, studied or slacked off.

It became a standing joke:

A = Awesome [I love 10s]
B = Good [9s are good]
C = Okay, not great [8s are okay]
D = Trouble [7s ehh]
F = Pow! [6s hospital]

In Moldova, they don't use the A through F system. They use a 10, 9, 8 . . . grading system.

We'd all laugh, but there was a serious undertone to all the joking. Someone had to encourage these children to focus on their studies, or they'd never have a chance in life. The orphanage workers had no use for encouragement; their teachers didn't care.

In my heart, I was Dad, and keeping the children focused on their grades was a very important part of the job.

As the kids lined up over and over and the months went by, I started to see improvement. Just as I cared about their grades, they began to care as well. It warmed my heart to see the extra effort they were investing.

One day we were in the lobby talking, and one of the older girls, Marina, motioned us upstairs where several of the girls were standing, talking, and giggling.

Pointing us to the chairs in the middle of the room, they asked Chrissie and me to sit.

"What do your kids call you?" Tania asked. "Well, they call me Dad."

"And Chrissie, what do they call her?"

"They call her Mom."

Immediately, the girls started chatting among themselves in Romanian. Finally, Tania piped up, "Can we call you Mom and Dad?" I am rarely speechless, but in that moment, I was at a complete loss for words. You see, I'd never told the kids what God had spoken to me.

I'd been doing everything in my power to be their dad, but I'd never said the word.

Never in my life have I felt as I did in that moment. A year had passed since the Lord said, "Be their dad." Now the kids were asking me the same thing.

Chapter 15
The Valley of the Shadow of Death

September in Southern Alabama always comes as a welcome relief from the scorching summer sun. The heat becomes more manageable. The kids are back in school. There is more order to life than the chaos of summer with four kids.

Even though I was supposed to be coming home early from work, I was running late that day, keenly aware that Chrissie would have lunch ready to put on the table before I could possibly get there.

I hated to be late. The kids were planning to attend youth group at church that evening, so family time would be limited to a quick meal, followed by taking turns chauffeuring the kids around town. I walked in the door to find Chrissie running behind as well, a rare thing.

With a few minutes to spare, I sat down in my chair and turned on the television. The phone beside me rang. As the sound filled the room, I suddenly flashed back to the day my dad had called me twenty-two years ago. And just as that phone call had changed the course of my life, so did this one.

"Hel—"

"You have to come," my mother's voice came across the line before the word was even out of my mouth. "You have to come now. Your dad is very sick. I just left him at the hospital. He is having trouble with his heart. Can you come tomorrow?"

My mother has never been one to overreact about anything. Calm was her middle name. And she never asks for anything. I knew if she was asking me to come, it was serious.

I spoke to her for only a few minutes, checking my watch and assuring her I would be on the next flight, knowing I could catch a red-eye to Scotland if I hurried. Within minutes of hanging up with my mother, I called Lisa Crews and told her to book the flight.

I grabbed the first clothes I saw and stuffed them into my well-traveled suitcase. I kissed Chrissie and the kids, rushed out to the car, and put it in gear. I was only a few miles from the house when my cell phone rang. It was Lisa.

"Philip, I just got off the phone with your brother in Scotland," she said. "It's not as bad as your mom seemed to think. Your dad will be fine. He'll be in the hospital for a few days, but you don't need to rush over there tonight. Really."

Her words tempted me. It would be so easy to cancel the flight, turn my car around, and go home to a nice meal. I'd been on the road so much lately, and I really wanted time at home with my family, but I felt a stirring in my spirit telling me not to turn around.

"No, I need to go now," I said to Lisa. "Thanks for checking, but I really need to go now. I'll call you tomorrow."

It was morning when I landed in Scotland, and the crisp fall air woke me up as I walked out of Aberdeen Airport with my mom. She looked tired and fragile, nothing like the strong woman I was used to seeing.

She and my dad were more than husband and wife—they really were soul mates. They finished each other's sentences. They completed each other. I could not imagine her without him, or him without her. Slowly walking to the car, she leaned into my shoulder as I put my arm around her. Words weren't needed. Together we prayed without saying a word.

The hospital in Aberdeen is a modern facility on the far end of town. I walked into the building, and the smells of disinfectant and medicine washed over me. The hospital was for sick people, and my dad was always the strongest person I knew—a powerhouse. What was he doing in this place? I had to admit to myself, he had never been quite the same since his surgery to remove the cancer from his back years ago, but still, this was Dad. He had to be okay.

I found his room on the third floor, right across from a noisy nurses' station. Without knocking, I walked in, and he looked at me with surprise.

"What are you doing here? Am I sicker than anyone told me?" he asked. I assured him he would be fine.

"Well, then, I hope you got a cheap ticket over here," he countered.

"Well, as a matter of fact, the ticket cost me one thousand dollars," I bantered back.

"I am worth it," he said with a hint of his famous smile.

I smiled back. On the inside, I was anything but smiling. He was swollen with fluid, his skin was a sick shade of yellow, and the pain was visible on his face. His kidneys were failing, and it caused his back to ache until it was almost unbearable. Still, he kept at me.

"So, what are the plans? When are you going back to Moldova? What is the news? What are you doing right now for Jesus?" Dad asked.

I found a chair and pulled up close to his bed. He knew every project and every child almost as well as I did. Although he was only able to make a few trips, he was forever on the phone with me, walking me through each situation, helping with challenges, poking holes in my strategies. And he loved the children. He loved to hear about our time with them, how their health improved, the joy we were starting to find in their hearts.

As I detailed the latest events, he'd respond, "Aye. Aye. That's good, mi' boy. Aye."

But each word pained him.

When I finished my report, I excused myself and stepped out to the nurses' station.

"Do you know when the doctor may be around?" I asked the nurse at the desk. "I'd like to talk to him."

Nodding, she pointed down the hall to the left. There he stood, looking over a chart, a young man in his early thirties. I walked over at once.

"Doctor, I am Simon Cameron's eldest son, Philip. I've just stepped off an overnight flight and I am very worried about him; I have never seen him like this. His kidneys don't seem to be working at all, he's full of fluid, and the pain is almost unbearable. Could you hook him up to a dialysis machine overnight, give his kidneys a break, and take some of the fluid pressure off his heart? It would help."

He stopped me cold. "You are kidding, right? Your dad is seventy-one. We don't have the money to be spending on giving him dialysis," he said, shaking his head and walking off without another word.

Universal health care had stolen the decisions about care from the hands of the Scottish doctors, and they stopped fighting it years ago. Now, it was all about money, return on investment. Perhaps for a younger man, they would do the treatment, but a seventy-one-year-old? Forget it.

I chased the man down the hall, barely catching him at the elevator. "But, Doctor, you don't understand. That is a very important man in that room," I said, pointing down the hall. "He is known all over the world as an evangelist, he has a Bible college, he has helped orphans all over Eastern Europe."

Before I could finish, he cut me off. "I am sorry," he said, the apology ringing hollow and false in my ears. He stepped in the elevator and pushed the button, and the conversation was over.

When I returned to the room, Dad's eyes were closed. Mom was holding his hand. Aside from the creaking sound the door made as it closed, the room was quiet. After a moment, Dad opened his eyes and looked at me.

"Son, I need you to pray for me. Pray for your dad."

I nodded my head and stood there awkwardly. Even as I write these words, I look back on that moment with regret. Did he mean "pray with me," as in the prayers that he knows I do all day, or did he mean he wanted me to lay hands on him and pray aloud for him right then and there?

I wish I could say I prayed out loud for him in that sterile hospital room, but all I could do was put my arm around my mom and wait until he drifted off into a fitful sleep. It was late; we stayed all day at the hospital after I had flown all night. I was tired to the bone and ready for bed. It seemed I had just fallen asleep, and I was being shaken by my mom. "Philip, get up. John has just been at the hospital in an ambulance run. He stopped by to see Dad, and he is fighting for his life. He just called me. We've got to get back to Aberdeen immediately." My brother-in-law John works as a paramedic in the ambulance service in our corner of Scotland. By chance he had taken a patient into the hospital and dropped by to see how dad was doing. He walked into the middle of a full-blown medical emergency. We raced through the night to Aberdeen. I've never driven so fast, yet thirty miles seemed like a hundred. I will never forget the knot in my stomach, the dread in my heart as we ran toward his room.

But it was too late. He died at 1:00 a.m. It was September 11, 2002.

An hour later, we were gathered around his hospital bed, my mom, my sisters Wendy and

Louise and my brother Neil. My brother-in-law John had never left his side. It was surreal. How could this man who had been the foundation of my life be gone? He was the only man whose approval I had ever needed. Gone. How would I know what to do next? If I was doing it right? I felt as helpless as a child. The next few days were a blur. Dad, in his three-piece suit, was in his coffin in the living room, as is the tradition in Scotland. Relatives came from all over, as did preachers, former students, and friends. I remember none of their words of condolence.

As my brother and I along with John and some of his grandsons carried him out to be buried, they played a recording I made of my Dad years ago: "Yea, though I walk through the valley of the shadow of death, I will fear no evil, for Thou art with me . . ." (Psalm 23:4, KJV).

Once his body was lowered into the ground, my spirit began to stir. I knew what I had to do. I knew what he would be saying to me if he was still with us: "What are you doing today, my boy? What are you doing for Jesus?"

I turned my grief into action, making plans, even as I was still in Scotland, to return to Moldova within a few weeks. There was much to do, and I knew, beyond a shadow of a doubt, that Simon was now watching, praying for me. I had to stay busy.

More and more, Cupcui became the focal point of my trips to Moldova, the needs of the children there more pressing. But on the way, we always stopped by Hincesti to see the other kids.

As we pulled up, I remember commenting how different even the outside of the building looked. It was nothing like the "dying rooms" I first encountered years ago.

We pulled up, and the kids ran to the windows to see who was there. "Feeleep! Feeleep!" they called, their accents thick (making my name sound more like "Feeleep"), rushing into my arms as they had before. I had watched these children grow up, knew almost all of them by name.

I tried to smile at the children while we finished delivering the gifts, but I was hurting. As soon as we could manage, we were back on the road.

On my next visit to Cupcui, I started asking the older girls what their plans were after they aged out of the orphanage, how they would survive.

I know the heart and life of an orphan in Moldova. These children are raised in a world where no decision is their own. From day one in the orphanage, they are told, "This is your bed. This is your shirt, your jeans. Eat this. Go to bed now. Today it is your turn to take a shower." You've read how cruel and cold the orphanage workers are; children are beaten often with no cause. At school, they are made fun of and told that they are less than nothing, and therefore deserve nothing because they are orphans.

What are they supposed to do on the outside? They are not educated beyond the ninth grade and lack the skills necessary to even boil an egg. One night in our little house, Chrissie asked the girls who were staying with us what they wanted to be when they left the orphanage. To our utter amazement they each had the identical answer: bucataria. I knew this word. I had just spent a small fortune replacing the decrepit equipment in the orphanage kitchen or bucataria. Chrissie asked again. "What do you want to do?" Again, the answer came: bucataria. I was incredulous. How could all these girls want to work in a kitchen? I pressed them further. Their answer broke my heart. "If we work in a kitchen, we will have food and it will be warm." I was stunned. These amazing kids full of so much promise had been limited in their thinking to the very basics of survival.

I knew that the June after they turn sixteen, orphans are sent away, but where would they go?

They couldn't go home to their families, of that I was certain. Obviously, if they had family members who loved them and could care for them, they would not be at the orphanage in the first place.

My children in Montgomery were raised to believe they could be anything they put their minds to. Doctors, lawyers, preachers, engineers—they could do it if they did the work. They had a future.

These kids had no concept whatsoever of a future beyond the basics to survive. A job in a kitchen was the very best they could hope for, dream of.

What these girls didn't know was that the unemployment rate was 70 percent in this part of the country. Their ninth-grade educations would not qualify them for anything, and as scorned orphans, they would be the last to be considered for any position, even if there was an opening.

So what would happen to them? What had already happened to the girls who had aged out last year and the year before?

I started asking the directors, the government officials, and I began reading articles online about what happens. It seemed that the government had decided that it was only obligated to care for orphans until they turn sixteen, so that was the law of the land. The June after every orphan's sixteenth birthday, the teenagers are given a few dollars and a bus ticket back to the village from which they came.

So a girl like Galina would be given a bus ticket to Chisinau, a two-hour bus trip to the capital city, and then she would take another bus to the village from which she had come on the other side of the country.

She would travel alone, with all that she owned in a plastic bag or cardboard box, terrified, not knowing how to survive.. With just a few clicks of the mouse, I learned about this routine. It is as well-documented as any policy, and, believe me, the sex traffickers know it as well. It just makes sense. Moldova is known as the engine of the sex trafficking machine, and no one is more vulnerable than a sixteen-year-old beautiful orphan girl.

To make matters worse, the workers in the orphanage often will tip off the traffickers with a call that alerts them, "I just put four Olympic-quality girls on the bus to Chisinau." For that, they will be rewarded more than a month's pay.

I learned that more than four hundred thousand women and girls had simply vanished from Moldova.

Some were kidnapped. Others were lured by stories of fake jobs in foreign countries. As soon as they were in a trafficker's care, all hope was lost. They would be out of the country and sold for as little as $3,500.

They would be drugged and beaten until they submitted to being used thirty to fifty times a day, making $350,000 a year for the trafficker. It was easy money for him. It was safer than selling drugs, easier than selling drugs. A little girl, once she is beaten, won't fight back.

Less than 1 percent of these girls ever escape, and even if they do, they are emotionally damaged for life. How does someone ever heal from that?

All of a sudden, I looked at the girls at Cupcui differently. I was their dad. I had to do something.

Then I had an idea that could have come only from God: We will build a house for the girls who are aging out and have it ready by June. We will feed them, we will allow them to finish school, we will protect them, and we will show them the love of Jesus every single day.

Chapter 16
A Home for Them

As this goes to press, combating sex trafficking is the cause du jour, and I agree that it should be—not just today, but for a long time.

But the majority of high-profile ministries and nonprofits are spending most of their money on raising awareness (whatever that means), on rescuing (though less than 1 percent of the girls who are rescued stay out of prostitution—out of options or so broken that they return to this terrible life), and on short rehab programs by people with good intentions.

Here is the problem I faced. I am a father, not just to my four kids, but to the dozens of kids I was raising who were living in orphanages. I was suddenly aware that these orphans practically had targets drawn on their backs. But what was I going to do about it? How could I protect them from this nightmare?

They needed a place to go, a real home in which to live. They needed to finish their education, literally grow up and learn to live and function as members of a family.

I needed to open a home—a big one—but I had no clue how to do it, and I didn't have the money to make it happen.

Frankly, the younger the orphans are, the easier it is to find money to help them. Gathering money for abandoned and abused puppies and kittens is easier, too, but we won't go there. It's almost impossible to raise money to help teenagers; countless other nonprofits and ministries have tried, but the assumption is that teens are old enough to take care of themselves. If only that were true.

I prayed. I sought counsel. I asked people in Moldova whom I trusted. Finally, I came up with a plan.

We would open a home for these girls in the city, allowing them to finish high school and then go on to vocational school or college. Chrissie and I would come and spend as much Mom and Dad time as we could, but we'd also hire a houseparent/missionary to be there twenty-four seven. The girls would do chores, like cooking and cleaning, skills they needed for a lifetime, and that would reduce our operational costs. All I needed to do was clear the plan with the government.

You would think that a plan and proposal for a nonprofit to open a home to protect aged-out sixteen-year-old orphans from sex traffickers would be met with cheers of joy from these cash-strapped officials.

"Mr. Cameron, what are you thinking?" a frightening-looking woman with badly dyed red hair and an ugly beige suit asked me. "These orphans are no longer our concern. We have fed them, educated them, put a roof over their heads. Our job is over. It is their time to become useful members of society now. We have other pressing needs. Real issues. Don't make this a problem for us."

That answer was not good enough for me. I kept trying other agencies, other towns, other levels of government. Soon, I became like the woman in the Bible with the unjust judge. I would not leave this alone. I would not take no for an answer. I had to protect these kids.

Finally, I was sitting in the well-appointed office of the governor of the area. Two young assistants were busy bringing us cookies and strong, bitter coffee.

He had granted me audience because I had given so much food and coal to the local orphanages. I had solved a problem for him. He didn't care about the children, but as long as I was helping with the orphans, it meant he had fewer issues with which to deal.

I sat in front of him, knowing how hard the hearts of these officials are. Children are of no value to them, and orphaned children mean even less.

Still, I tried to appeal to him from one father to another. Surely he knew as well as I did the nightmare that each one of these girls would face. He was unmoved.

I kept talking. I tried to look sincere and nonthreatening. In the simplest of terms, I told him what we would offer the girls—food, clothes, an education, life skills.

"Education?" he stopped me midsentence. "Education?"

It seemed I had landed on the one thing Communists are big on providing.

Yes, we would guarantee to keep these girls in school. So we struck a deal that I could take the girls in as long as they were in school while they were in our organization's care. Some would be still in high school, some would be in vocational tech training, while others would be going to university. But they had my word that every girl would remain in school.

The plan started to come together. If the girls lived in the city, it meant that there was public transportation to take them to school. That was vital because the girls all would be on different schedules and in dozens of schools and colleges scattered about Chisinau. Transporting them in our own vans was not an option.

We started looking for an appropriate house and were floored by the price of real estate! Our needs were very specific; I wanted a house large enough for the girls who would age out of Cupcui in just a few weeks. We had no time to lose, but it had to be in a safe area where we could provide good security.

The process of building in Moldova was different from anything I had ever encountered. The country had no banking system, and no one could take out a mortgage to buy a home. Instead, people bought land and, as they had the money, would build homes in stages.

All over town there are shells of houses made of stone and cement—nothing but the basement, floors, and partial walls. Sometimes there are roofs. The shells are left like this for years and even decades until the family has the money to build more or decides to sell.

We looked at countless shells all over the city before we found the right place.

Garth Coonce, a great giant of faith, was with me on that trip. He had been my friend for many years. The founder of TCT Ministries, Garth had brought twenty-four-hour Christian television to many towns that had never had easy access to the gospel on television.

Garth is a dear, dear friend and a brilliant businessman. Seeing this shell, knowing the need, he gave us one hundred thousand dollars to get started on the project as soon as we walked the site. He knew in his spirit that it was right for us, just as I did.

His gift was the miracle—and the encouragement—I needed to pull out all the stops to make this a reality.

We had the funds to buy the shell, now came the bigger task of finishing the home. Miracle after miracle took place as I traveled itinerating in what seemed a myriad of churches. Little by little we saw a shell turn into a home. It was time to bring some orphans home. We brought the girls from the orphanage and welcomed them to the only real home they had ever known. My daughter, Melody, decorated and appointed it as nice as my home in Montgomery. These girls were no longer orphans; they were my children, so why would I give them anything less?

One of the finest days of my life was the day I gave those first girls a tour of what would be their new home. I watched with tears in my eyes as they discovered a thousand things that made this place a home—not a warehouse for children, like they were used to. Everything was clean, and small trinkets and pictures on the walls gave each room character.

There were no more than three girls to a room, giving them the space and privacy that they had never had. The beds were made with matching brightly colored comforters, soft pillows, firm mattresses, things they had never seen in their lives. They even had drawers and closets, furnishings they had never needed because they owned nothing.

But what really got their attention was the kitchen. There was no lock on the door. They were allowed in at any time. They could make a sandwich or snack any time of the day. They could choose what food to eat and when to eat. These were all unheard-of concepts at the orphanage!

"When I first walked into the house, I thought I was dreaming," Galina said of her first time she was at the house. "It was the most amazing thing. I never had to share my bed with anybody or wake up in the middle of the night to move my bed because of the leaking problems we had at our orphanage before Dad fixed it."

I shared my faith when asked, but I did not force any of the girls to go to church or read the Bible. I was purposeful in not putting a television in the house, bringing one out only on special occasions. The Jesus film was one of several movie options, along with other carefully selected films.

Like in any home, we had rules. They had to stay in school (and do well), they had to share chores with the others, and they had to learn to function as a family.

The girls had homework and chores. For their fun, I wanted them interacting with one another, playing games, sharing their days, being a family.

When one of the new girls asked why I did this for them—and they all asked—I answered, "Because of all God has done for me." Their questions allowed me to share my faith at their pace. When they asked for a Bible, I was ready with one. When they wanted to visit a church, we had the van ready to take them.

I watched these girls transform, both spiritually and emotionally, some almost overnight, some more slowly. When you are raised as an orphan, you hold everything you are given close to you, willing to fight because of the fear of losing what precious little you own.

They slowly began to let down their guards. Over time, they began to relax in the knowledge that the clothes they were given were really theirs. No one would beat them or yell at them. They had been orphans together; now they were sisters.

They learned to share. They learned to trust. They learned what it was to be loved unconditionally. And with that, one at a time, they asked Jesus to be their Lord and Savior.

I never told them to start Bible studies, but they did. I never told them to pray together, to share their scars, their dreams, their lives with one another, but they did. Never in my life have I seen any group of kids turn a vague concept of God into such a deep, abiding relationship with Jesus Christ. It took my breath away!

Early on, I learned that these kids never complain. If they are sick with the flu, or even something much more serious, they keep it to themselves. The workers at the orphanage had trained and conditioned them that no one cares if they are sick or hurting. No one comes if you are crying at night. There were no trips to doctors, no over-the-counter medications to ease symptoms; if you were sick, too bad.

But Galina had concerned me for some time, and her problem with her eyes was getting worse and worse. Glasses had helped, but I knew there was a deeper problem. Her vision was darkening, her headaches were more acute, and her dizzy spells seemed to come out of nowhere.

In Moldova, there is so-called universal health care, but orphans are in their own lowly class. I finally found a private doctor who would see her. After a battery of tests, a scan confirmed that she had a benign brain tumor that was pressing on the nerve behind her eye. It was inoperable and progressive. He could give her pain pills but suggested that she drink a lot of wine instead.

Galina was crestfallen. In the hallway, I gave her a hug and assured her this was not the end of the story. Like any dad, I was going to do whatever I could to see my little girl healed.

"Next stop," I told her, "will be the embassy. We will get you a visa, and I will find a doctor in America who will operate on you and get that tumor gone. I promise. Start praying for favor at the embassy and the right doctor to step forward to help you."

We brought Galina over to the States on a medical visa. The first thing a doctor did was give her an eye test and fit her with a new pair of glasses. I was so happy for her, but remembered all the tears she had shed struggling to do homework when she could not see the blackboard at school. All those wasted years, all because an orphan was not worth taking to an eye doctor!

Next we saw a surgeon who confirmed and documented the exact size and position of the tumor. Yes, it was progressive, but he could remove it. He had operated on much more complex ones than this, and he waived his fee. He gave her medication that would help her symptoms and pain and explained the need to wait a few months to do the surgery, but said that in less than a year, if all went well, she would be healed.

Galina didn't know what to say. She had hardly gotten used to the fact that she could see with glasses. Now there was hope, a plan for the headaches to be taken care of. No more dizziness? No more struggling to get through each day? It was almost more than she could bear. "I was very nervous about the surgery," Galina later recalled. "I was very nervous that something could go wrong, that I could end up paralyzed."

Although I was happy and smiling on the outside, I have to confess that I was worried too. Brain surgery. The thought of them putting her to sleep and drilling into her brain was a frightening thought. Yes, I knew doctors performed surgeries all the time, but this was our girl! It was different.

I left her with Chrissie and the other four kids at home and continued the work as we waited for the surgery.

At the same time, I had started a construction project at another orphanage called Straseni. A government official came to the house we were building and "asked" if I would come with her to see an orphanage in dire straits. I learned that it was the largest orphanage in Moldova. It housed eight hundred children, just a short drive from Chisinau, the capital city. While I didn't physically have the time to invest in getting to know all the children as well as I had come to know the kids at Cupcui, when I discovered the place and saw how terrible the windows were, knowing winter was coming, I had to act.

Turning to the director, I asked, "How many windows do you need?"

"I think one hundred," he said. He looked at his shoes. "Maybe two hundred." Another pause. "Perhaps three hundred."

In all, it took 391 windows to protect the eight hundred children in this orphanage from the danger of freezing to death. On top of the house we had just finished, I knew it was impossible to go back and ask people who had already sacrificed to give me the funds to supply all of these windows. I was speaking at The Refuge Church in Concord, NC. Pastor Jay Stewart had been heroic in his support of our work in Moldova. I was almost embarrassed to bring such a huge challenge so soon after they had helped with the house we had just finished. A few weeks after we had been to his church we met in Huntsville, Alabama. We were both on the board of the Rock Church pastored by Rusty Nelson. During that board meeting Jay mentioned to me that he wanted to talk about the windows in Straseni. I felt sick in my stomach. I had tried desperately to raise this money to no avail. The last thing I wanted Jay to do was to tell me that he had enough money to buy four or five windows. In fact, the day before I had told my office staff that I had given up on the "windows." Now here he was about to complicate a situation that had already defeated me. The total cost for these windows was $170,000. There was a pause in the meeting, and Jay made a beeline towards me. "Philip you won't believe what happened the other day. A man came to my office and challenged me to help you with these windows. He has given $100,000 on the condition that the church match his gift. We have taken the rest of the money from our building fund. We desperately need a new church. These kids need windows more." I was flabbergasted. I had just learned another lesson in the economy of heaven. These kids belonged to God. If I were interested in helping them, He was much more so. We will never be able to thank LC Lynch and pastor Jay Stewart and the amazing folks at The Refuge for coming to the rescue for me and the kids in Moldova. I only wish I hadn't told my office staff about giving up on the windows. If I had kept quiet another day, I would have been a hero. Instead I had to go back and expose my lack of faith to those who worked with me.

On a sunny June afternoon, Chrissie and I dropped by to see how the completion of the windows had gone, to make sure everything was in order. The director gave me a tour, pleased to show me the finished work. It was amazing. These young lives would never again be threatened by winter's icy fingers. Many nights snow would blow into the rooms forcing them to huddle as many as could together in a bed trying to keep warm and avoid freezing to death.

As we returned to his office, the thankful director thought he might push his luck even further. "Come with me, I want to show you something." Outside I saw eighteen teenage girls sitting and standing around a blue bench in front of the orphanage building. Every one of them was dressed in ratty jeans and a tee shirt and spotted with whitewash paint.

He waved his arm at them, "They all must go," he told me. "All of them are sixteen this year. Today was the last day of school. They are just finishing painting their rooms for the new kids we will soon take in." Horror washed over me.

Eighteen girls with no place to go. I couldn't look away from their innocent faces. I knew what awaited them; they had no clue. It was like seeing a child running after a ball into the street and into an oncoming car that until then had gone unseen. I had to stop this nightmare, but how?

I turned to my wife and said, "Chrissie, how many girls could we take in the new house?"

She was quiet for a moment as she turned the idea over in her mind. She looked at me, her face turning pale at the horror of what was unfolding. "Three is the most we could take. Every bed is already taken, but if we don't have a computer room three beds could be put in there."

I looked back at the faces before me. Innocent. Beautiful. Alone. How could I pick three? What would happen to the other fifteen? My heart cried to the Lord. This was so unfair. How could I pick three and condemn the others to hell on earth?

It was impossible. I told the director not to send them away yet, that we would be back the next day. At 8:00 the following morning, I was back as promised, but with some of the girls from Cupcui. I made them choose.

"Talk to the girls. Find out who is willing to work hard to have a future. You have to pick just three more sisters."

And they did.

I don't know how the girls managed to choose three of the eighteen girls on that bench, but they did. They took the decision very seriously, welcoming in three girls who were willing and able to work hard for a successful future. Every day I think about the girls whom I was forced to turn away. Every day my heart is burdened by that horrible day. But I have been so blessed by the three girls who joined our family that day.

While more reserved about her feelings, Dasa- one of the three chosen that day- told me, matter-of-factly, the overview of her story.

"My earliest memory is being marched outside with my three cousins," she told me. "It was very hot. My auntie's husband threatened to hit us if we didn't kneel down on some hard, dry kernels of corn while he screamed at us. He was angry at my aunt for leaving us alone with him."

Every day was filled with fear for the tiny blonde girl. She slept in the bed with her cousins and awoke many nights to the terrifying sounds of her aunt being beaten. "Please don't kill me," she would beg while the children cowered in their beds.

It was a blessing to the kids when her uncle was arrested as a thief and sent to prison. Life had just started to seem better when suddenly, the other adults decided to leave the country for a "better life."

The children were left alone in the house for weeks at a time. Every few days one of her older cousins would come by to check on them.

"I would go in my mother's room, to her closet, and pull out her clothes and try to catch the smell of her," Dasa told me. "I wanted her to come home so badly."

Later on, her relatives decided to put all the children in the orphanage believing that this would give them a bit of stability in their life.

"Nothing was different in the orphanage," Dasa remembers. "I was still hungry all the time. I was alone. It was the same hopelessness."

Now, instead of a drunken uncle, Dasa had to deal with mean staff workers who would tell her, "You are nothing. An orphan is less than nothing. You will never be anything."

After five miserable years in the orphanage, it was almost time for Dasa to leave—not that she had anywhere to go.

After we took her into our care, Dasa blossomed into an outstanding young woman of faith. Today she is the main interface between our ministry in America and the work in Moldova and Ukraine. She speaks Russian, Romanian and English. Dasa has written two books and after attending Auburn University, graduating with honors, continues to be a leader in our ministry.

Chapter 17
Dasa's Cousin Andrei

The girls on the bench, the ones we had lost into the darkness, underscored the need to expand our ministry in Moldova. We needed room for more girls, and we needed it quickly.

A little more than two miles away, we found property on a safe side street. On the two-acre lot stood four shells of homes that had never been completed. If we could buy and finish them, we would be able to wall them off, providing an additional level of security, and provide a home for as many as 110 girls. But each of the shells was owned by a different family, and we hardly had the cash to buy all four at one time anyway. All we could do was buy one, complete it, and pray.

As we neared completion of the first home, I felt the Lord speaking to me through the girls. Many of them had brothers and cousins who had aged out at the same time as they had. These young boys were living on the streets, starving. Although they were not as much at risk for sex trafficking, there were countless reports of boys being enslaved and forced to work in construction in Russia under brutal conditions. Dasa had a cousin. His name was Andrei. The more she got to know me and her English understanding grew, there was something she continually was trying to tell me. This unlocked secret was driving her to learn to speak a foreign language so she could tell me what was burdening her heart. A few visits passed. Each visit this little blonde girl would look at me and try to explain something that I just couldn't understand. I had just arrived back in Moldova. The house was busy.

Laughter came from every room; Mom and Dad were back to see them. Chrissie was in the kitchen making them chicken and sweet corn soup. All was well. That is, except for Dasa. She sat beside me on the sofa and spoke in her best English, "Dad I have cousin. He is lost, nowhere to stay. Why not you have a house for boys?" Here she was barely saved herself yet she was reaching out of her circumstance trying to make a place at the table of hope for her cousin, whose mother had been killed when he was only five years old and whose father he had never known. Over the next days at every chance, this little girl would sit beside me and ask me again and again. "What about my cousin? Can you make house for him?" She had great compassion for a cousin who unknown to us was held in a work camp against his will. Andrei was exactly why we needed a house for boys. I couldn't shake it. I couldn't shake Dasa. By sheer determination she was making me make a decision to expand again and caused me to realize that these boys were mine, too. What would take you minutes to read took me two years to achieve. To build a house, a home for boys. As they came into their house, I saw the light of promise in their eyes, in their gifts, in their drive.

The day of the grand opening, my seventy-eight-year-old mother—the unsung hero behind everything my dad ever did—flew down from Scotland. She walked up the stairs, dressed to perfection, as always, with her perfect hair, her high-heeled shoes. She cut the ribbon to open the door and hung with care a large portrait of my dad in the living room of our first boys' home.

Chapter 18
America

Between the two homes and other orphanages, plus our ongoing ministry in the United States and in Scotland, I often woke up from nightmares. My worst possible dream was that one day I would not have enough money to keep the houses going, and I would have to turn these kids out onto the street.

When I wasn't in Moldova, I was raising money at different churches every Sunday, filling in with midweek services and camp meetings anytime I was booked. It was grueling, exhausting, but I loved to tell the stories of these kids and how much they mean to me. Time and time again, I experienced the power of the Holy Spirit as I spoke, and somehow the funds were always there (though barely).

The members of some churches got so excited that they made mission trips to Moldova to see the kids, to hear firsthand where they had come from and what God was doing in their lives. The results were always the same: Once people met these kids, they came to feel the way I did—protective, blessed, inspired, moved to tears.

I had to think that part of the reason it was so affective was that these girls and boys were not speaking through a translator. Most of them had taught themselves English, and they spoke with amazing clarity. Every raw emotion and feeling brought stories vividly to life, leaving nothing lost in translation.

I realized that I needed to bring some of the kids to the United States. They needed to tell their own story, to put a face and give a voice to the orphans in our care.

Like the process of adopting Andrew had been, the process of bringing the girls to the States was more complex and convoluted than I ever could put on these pages. I knew enough about immigration and visas to the United States to know that I could apply for the girls to visit in the summer months, when school was out, but I could not predict who would be allowed to come or for how long. We started with the kids who loved the Lord, whose English was good, who showed interest in making the trip, and who had the maturity to be trusted with a new level of responsibility.

Everyone who made that list filled out an application for a visa. We hired a lawyer and chatted up everyone we knew at the embassy. And then we waited.

Back in Alabama, I filled my days with more church visits, talking with at least one of the girls in Moldova every day. Everyone was waiting to find out who, if anyone, would be allowed to travel to the States for the summer.

I returned to Moldova in the middle of "mud season." It was almost Easter, and the winter winds had died down. It rained at least once a day, and the snowbanks were slowly melting. Water flowed from the hillside, and the soil had absorbed all that it could.

As much as I hated the snow, I hated the mud more. With every step, the mud would attempt to suck the shoes right off my feet, and if I somehow managed to get into the house with both still on, they were caked with thick dark mud that dried into what seemed to be brown concrete.

But I made it my practice to come to Moldova every year for Orthodox Easter, a week after we celebrated Easter in Alabama. It was a large and strange holiday in Moldova. Nothing like it is in America. Because kids often had strong emotions tied to the holidays from their childhood (good and bad), I always wanted to be there. More importantly, I wanted to replace what they knew of Easter with what it really is.

I loved to tell them the real Easter story, the story of Jesus, of His entrance into Jerusalem on Palm Sunday. The kids would hang on each word as I told them about the Last Supper, about when Jesus was arrested, and of His trial. Many would weep as I talked about our Savior being beaten and whipped until the flesh was torn away and His every bone and muscle was exposed. Then the cross, the nails, His mother at His feet.

With each telling, I would pause after I talked about the darkness that fell over the earth and our Lord simply saying, "It is finished," as He drew His last human breath.

Then came Sunday. I'd watch the kids' faces as I talked about the stone that was rolled away. He is risen! He is risen!

Yes, I loved to come on Easter and tell the story over and again. But this year, as we finished and conversations began to drift, the girls asked again about their visas. Would they be able to go to this country they had heard so much about? Could they meet the people who gave the money so that their home could exist? Could they help Dad by telling their story? I didn't know, and I hated telling them I had no control of the decisions or the timing. All we could do was pray.

One late afternoon we got their passports back from the embassy. Half were approved for entry into the United States, while the others were turned down flat with no explanation at all.

After studying the visas more carefully, I noticed that in many of the cases, two of the applications were exactly the same, other than the name—same age, same year in school, same amount of time with us, from the same orphanage—yet one would be approved, and one, denied. It seemed as if someone had thrown all of the applications in the air as hard as possible. When the applications floated down and landed on the floor, the ones facing up were stamped with a YES, and the ones facing down were stamped with a NO.

Surely it was not that random, but it sure appeared that way. I braced myself to deliver the news. It killed me that I had to say no to some of them, but what else could I do?

The girls were amazing when I shared the news. There were no tears from the ones who could not go, only hugs and shouts of joy for those who could.

As they celebrated, I broke away and called the office in Montgomery. We had only a few weeks to buy airline tickets, and it was vital that we all travel together. None of these girls would have a clue what to do if they were stranded overnight in Paris or Rome or some other gateway city.

When we arrived in the United States, the immigration officer asked each of the girls how long she planned to stay. Our girls all said, "Three months," knowing full well that the officer could refuse and write "three weeks," or even "three days," on the visa. It was nerve-racking, but all who made it into the States were approved for the three-month stay.

This became the first of many summer tours. I outfitted a used RV for the summer, and we set about across the country. We had a van filled with luggage, books, CDs, and other things we sold at churches, and my sons Philip Jr. and Andrew took turns driving. Chrissie and my two daughters, Melody and Lauren Ann rode with the girls and me in the RV.

At around midnight of the first day of our maiden tour, we stopped at an all-night diner to get something to eat. Except for a couple of highway troopers sipping coffee in the corner booth, the place was almost empty. A couple of the waitresses helped us push tables together, then passed out menus.

The chatter stopped as everyone stared at the menus in their hands. I was still deciding between the fish-and-chips (in Indiana, would any cook really know how to make fish-and-chips for a Scotsman?) and something they would be less likely to mess up—a hamburger, perhaps—when the waitress reappeared.

"What'll it be?" she asked, her pen poised over the order pad.

"Let the girls go first," I responded as I waved with my hand. "I'm still trying to decide. Galina? Anybody? Just start."

Silence.

I looked over my menu at the girls. A dozen pair of bewildered eyes stared back at me.

"Come on," I said, my irritation barely contained, "just start." It was Chrissie who finally broke the silence.

"Philip, I don't think they know," she said. "They can't read English and wouldn't know what these dishes are. Chicken fried steak? Cobb salad? Chicken and stuffing? They don't serve these things in Moldova, especially not in an orphanage."

And thus, began what I like to call the "Golden Corral Tour." For as long as these girls travel with us, we have to find as many buffets as possible. Then they can see potatoes, green beans, roast beef . . . whatever, and make up their own minds what to eat.

But the meals were just the beginning of the adventure. The services, of course, were the highlight of the trip. I learned very quickly to give the microphone over as often as possible to the girls and let them share from their hearts.

Each girl was remarkable in her own way. The congregations would look at these girls—girls who looked so much like those in their own youth groups, in their own homes. Out of the girls' innocent mouths, the congregations heard about what it felt like to starve. To be beaten. Hated. Abandoned.

One of our stops was Branson, Missouri, where my dear friend Jim Bakker had a daily television program. Jim had been special to my family and me since back in the early '70s when he and Tammy Faye had been at The 700 Club.

Over the years, he had changed and grown as he walked through the valley, losing PTL, being publicly humiliated, being sent to prison for what seemed to be a life sentence, his wife divorcing him, his kids getting in trouble.

But like the Bible promises, He is a God who restores. Jim's lovely wife, Lori, was a delight, and his ministry was growing and thriving.

Jim began to weep as the girls shared their stories on his program. As the audience realized that, as terrible as it is, this is a solvable issue, Jim changed his earlier plans for the show.

"We want to help build the next house," he announced. "Will you help me?"

For most of an hour, we talked and testified, and Jim repeated the need. When the taping ended, we had no idea if the show would be successful, since it would not air for a few days.

I knew Jim's ministry was struggling financially, and, in fact, there were days when he seriously thought of retiring to some small cottage in the woods and forgetting it all. After all, he was seventy years old.

But quitting has never been in Jim's nature any more than it was in my dad's. When God said, "Do it," Jim did it, and his willingness to do God's work was evidenced all around the ministry he had named Morningside. The television program was just a small part of what he was doing. Perhaps the ministry with the longest-lasting impact will prove to be the school to train young people in evangelism and communications called Morningside Masters Media.

Bright, spirit-filled kids from all over the country were there, learning to run cameras and produce their own programs. They lived on the grounds, prayed together, worked side by side, and had become an amazing force for the kingdom. The girls quickly captured their attention. When we weren't on air, they were together, just being kids. Kids who love the Lord.

Galina had been suffering a lot that week, the pain in her eyes almost unbearable. After receiving permission to take her from Moldova to the United States for surgery on the tumor, a second X-ray in Alabama revealed that the tumor was gone. I insisted that they redo the scan, over the objection of the doctor.

"I know it seems like a waste of time, but trust me," I pleaded with him. "I'll pay extra for it, but please do it."

Finally, he agreed. The girls and I anxiously waited for the results.

When Galina reached out and took my hand, she was smiling.

"I knew, because of how I was feeling, that something good was coming, and it did," she said.

She knew, before the doctor came back with the look of absolute astonishment on his face, that the tumor in her brain was gone, completely gone.

Although the tumor was gone, her eyesight was still blurry. She never complained to me, but I knew she was hurting. She was quieter than usual, more withdrawn, and I'd often catch her napping in the middle of the day.

Soon after, one of the girls from Master's Media noticed it, too, and began to ask pointed questions. Galina told the others the whole story, how she had suffered as a child not being able to see, but that there had never been a doctor to diagnose her, let alone even look at her.

"God can heal you," one of the students told Galina.

"Yes, yes," another agreed, and started sharing an amazing testimony of another healing that had happened at Morningside just weeks before. Another student started quoting God's Word about healing: "Matthew 9:22 says, 'Jesus turned and saw her. "Take heart, daughter," he said, "your faith has healed you." And the woman was healed at that moment,'" the student told Galina, quoting the NIV. "And then there's James 5:14: 'Is anyone among you sick? Let them call the elders of the church to pray over them and anoint them with oil in the name of the Lord.' We want to pray for you, Galina."

The students gathered around Galina, placing their hands on her. Boldly, these children of God stormed the gates of heaven on behalf of Galina; boldly they entered into His presence. Many were praying in unknown tongues. One girl was singing a song of praise and worship, an angelic voice covering the prayers of so many gathered in His name.

A strange warmness settled over Galina as they prayed. The pain in her head ebbed. Everything became fuzzy when she blinked her eyes. After blinking again, she was amazed to find that she could see better, but through her glasses, things were out of focus. She took them off, and her vision was immediately clear. She was able to see better than she had ever been able to see before in her entire life!

She began to laugh and to cry, telling the others what she was experiencing. All prayer turned to praise.

"I felt like the heaviness disappeared," she later told me. "I felt reborn, like a new person. It's something I can't even explain. Even today, it's amazing, something you can't forget."

Hours later we pulled out in our RV, and the girls were strangely silent. We all kept stealing glances at Galina, who sat off in the back, still with no glasses, a look of complete serenity on her face.

Between trips and services, the girls literally became part of our family. We put beds up in the attic so they could all stay in our house. Chrissie made chore charts for them to take turns helping her cook, shop, clean, and handle other household chores.

I made myself available as we were driving, as we waited for dinner, as we sat outside by the pool. It was in those hours that real healing began to take place for many of the girls. Details of their lives they had never told anyone came pouring out. Dreams. Fears. Questions.

By the time summer was over, we brought back to Moldova a very different group of girls from the ones we had brought to the States. They had all grown up. Their English was nearly perfect. They were grounded in their faith in a way that was breathtaking. They felt validated, important enough to travel, to take the message of the orphans to thousands and thousands of people. I was never prouder of them.

Chapter 19
Vatra Village

I was on my way to Straseni. Ten years had passed since the miracle of the windows. Many more kids had come to us and now were husbands and wives, mothers and fathers, and lived all over the world. I have so many photographs of beautiful "grandchildren," and almost daily my phone dings with pictures as they grow. As we drove, I noticed through the trees off to my right a village of the most beautiful homes. I had enough on my plate; I didn't need any more worry. Yet something drew me to this lovely spot about a hundred yards from Moldova's largest lake. "Pull over." I tapped Pavel, one of our house parents, on his shoulder. He quickly brought our van to a halt. "Over there, behind those trees, what are those houses all about?" Pavel shrugged. Without thinking he had turned into the drive that led to where my interest lay. Soon I was looking through the black iron fence to the six houses placed around a village green. They looked like they had been lifted from a village in Switzerland. I knew nothing about them other than that they were empty and unfinished. "Pavel, I want you to find out about these houses. Who owns them? Are they for sale? Can I see inside them?" I didn't realize that my curiosity had just put me on the path to massively expand our challenge to save more kids than ever before.

We had been looking in Ukraine. This unlikely turn of events was the result of a crazy meeting with an immigration officer in the Atlanta airport. Chrissie and I stood at his desk and went through the usual proceedings that I had gone through hundreds of times.

"Where have you been?"

"Moldova."

His head snapped upward. He fixed me in his gaze. "Where?"

"Moldova," I said, both of us suddenly interested in what normally is a very mundane event.

"Moldova?" he asked again. I didn't get a chance to answer. "This is crazy. You won't believe what I am about to tell you." I had no idea that an immigration officer in Atlanta airport would send me on another rescue mission. "I just transferred up from the Caribbean," he began. "While there we intercepted a forty-foot container from Odessa, Ukraine. Inside there were forty girls, all of them from Moldova!" He thanked me for helping the girls who were subject to this horrendous fate. The long line behind me brought our interchange to a close. He stamped our passports and thanked me again. I left with a burdened heart. As we waited for our suitcases, I looked at Chrissie and without a word being spoken, she knew.

Odessa, Ukraine is a bitterly cold place in January. Snow was thick and getting thicker by the hour. I thought we would end up being stuck in this freezing place. My son Andrew, Pavel and some of the young people from Moldova were with us. We were looking for a home where we could put "our finger" in the dam that was being overwhelmed by the curse of trafficking. I had decided to move two of our house parents, Oleg and Elena, from Moldova to the new home we had found in Odessa. Pavel's phone rang. He spoke in Romanian and turned toward me. "Dad, it is a representative of the owners of the houses we saw on our way to Straseni. He wants to meet with you this afternoon."

"Pavel, how can he meet with us when I am in Ukraine and he is in Moldova?"

Pavel smiled. "He's not in Moldova. He has been driving all day to meet you here." He had arranged to meet me in the most ironic of places. In the center of Odessa there is a Scottish restaurant with a man in a kilt.

I laughed at Pavel. "It would take a miracle for someone to drive from Moldova to Odessa in this weather."

Pavel replied: "He will call when he gets close."

He did, and I went to meet him. I walked past the statue of the kilted warrior into the dark restaurant and shook the representative's hand and sat down across the table. He began, "I am here to offer you the houses beside the lake in Vatra."

I interrupted him. "Before you begin," I began, "I know about this village. I know how much they were sold for previously and I am not prepared to pay you more than a million dollars for the property."

Now it was his turn to interrupt me. "I know. They know." Vatra village had been bought previously by another organization. They had been unable to maintain the monthly payments and it had been foreclosed. "Here is what they want to offer you. The money they had received previously will be counted against the original price. They will sell you the buildings for fifty percent of the original."

Now it was my turn to have my breath taken away. I was up to my neck in Odessa. We were committed to supporting the houses in Moldova, saying my plate was full was a gross understatement. In a second an answer came, from where I don't know. I heard my voice speaking, but it felt as if someone else was using my voice. "It's a deal." My hand shot out to grasp his. We had committed ourselves to the biggest challenge in our history.

The Odessa was open. Young girls were being rescued and raised to know Jesus by Oleg and Elena. It was both exciting and terrifying. I never thought it was possible to have dreams and nightmares in the same night. My spirit saw the possibility; my natural mind shuddered at the thought of such a huge challenge. I flew home almost afraid to tell Chrissie and the rest of the team what I had just done.

My phone dinged. I was in my easy chair trying to recover from jetlag. Only those who travel understand the agony of this phenomena. I picked up the phone. It was a photograph from a dear friend, Marcus Lamb. I opened the message and looked at the picture. Marcus, Joni, President Trump and Melania were smiling from my phone. Marcus was with the president. I instantly replied, "That ain't no big deal, I just bought a village!" I waited to see if he would respond. In a few seconds my phone dinged again. "Daystar Television Network will sponsor one of your homes." I hadn't had the chance to even explain how much it would cost for a house. I almost fell off my chair. Marcus Lamb, a life-long friend, had just given the foundation gift that would begin a domino effect that literally took my breath away. I had been home for less than an hour and God was already answering my prayer. His incredible gift would motivate others in major ministries to believe with me for the most incredible dream of my life.

The next day I was back in the office. I had called Dasa along with a bunch of other people the night before. There was a new challenge. How do we begin transforming these unfinished shells into the homes we had dreamed about? Dasa made a suggestion. "Let's call Nadia." Nadia was another miracle in Dasa's life. The day we chose three girls at Straseni orphanage, Nadia was left on the bench. She had tried to find accommodation and had to settle for a dormitory that was one step away from the hell of trafficking. At night she could not sleep because of the "activity" that filled the dorm each night. During the day she had tried to focus on her studies, but exhaustion would rob her focus and attention. She fell behind. The same Dasa that had begged me to help her cousin Andrei was back at it again, telling me about her cousin that I had overlooked that day on the bench. "Dad, please help my cousin Nadia. She is in a dangerous place. Can she come to be with me in my room?" Unknown to me Dasa would take some of her food and go by bus to meet her cousin and share with her enough to keep

Nadia from starving. As with Andrei, the little "Esther" pleaded her case, and she too became part of our family. We put her in university where she studied interior design, which included the foundation of building homes. Seeds that we had sown years before were about to become the answer to our dilemma.

Dasa called Nadia and explained about Vatra, and Nadia became the main contractor to finish the homes at Vatra Village. This amazing girl in a chauvinist world has saved our ministry tens of thousands of dollars. Arguing, cajoling, negotiating with builders and suppliers to create the most exquisite homes for orphans you have ever seen. Vatra Village was built to be occupied by wealthy people. Situated on the largest lake in Moldova, these homes were built to be summer "dachas" of the upper class in what ironically is meant to be, according to the communist dogma, a classless society. We were able to pay for the village with the help of TCT Television Network, CTN Television Network, Elevate Life Church in Frisco, Texas, and a multitude of hearts that heard our vision, gave and made the most incredible miracle take place in what has been called the "saddest country on earth."

Three years had passed since that snowy day in Odessa. Two containers from the US had arrived in Moldova. Chrissie, my daughter Melody, Andrew and myself had gone to meet them and have Christmas with our kids at Vatra Village. It was evening as we approached the same place as I had caused Pavel to stop so many years earlier. That day the windows of these houses looked back at us with empty stares. I had peered through the dirty windows into raw plastered rooms where damp and leaks from destroyed roofs had allowed water to pour into the empty space.

We turned into the driveway. The cold mist of a Moldovan winter had drifted up from the lake and had isolated each house from the other by a white blanket. Tonight was different. As our car came to a gentle stop beside the village green around which these houses stand, my heart overflowed as I looked to the same windows that now had the glow of home. I climbed out of the car and heard the laughter of so many voices. Hearts that had found a home. *Vatra* translated into English means "hearth." I didn't choose the name Vatra. It was on the maps before I got there. But somehow, I feel a loving Father, an eternal loving Father looked down on that place and in His Divine plan decided to make a home for the lost souls that no one else had wanted. Thousands of miles separated me from where I lived. Alabama is almost six thousand miles from Vatra Village. Yet as I stood in the mist, I had never felt more at home. Truly, home is where the heart is.

Chapter 20
Outreach Center

It was January 7; we had rented a little church to hold our Christmas party. In Moldova, Christmas is celebrated on this date because of the dominance of the Russian Orthodox Church. However, more recently, the January Christmas is losing ground to the December date. I guess tradition can't compete with the West. It suits us; we can enjoy Christmas in America with our family, then as the New Year turns, we head East to enjoy Christmas all over again with those God has placed in our hearts, not of blood but most certainly of spirit. They sang, played games, told the Christmas story. As a surprise Chrissie and I sang, and they cheered. Most didn't know I've spent most of my life being known as a singer. Then my daughter Melody and "Mom" went to the huge pile of boxes covered in a myriad of colored paper. This is one of the greatest labors of love I've ever seen. From the moment the container of Christmas gifts leaves from our warehouse in a forty-foot container, Chrissie begins again for the next year. Every night, up in the craft room in our home, she pulls together the gifts for the next Christmas. She knows each of the kids' favorite colors, sizes, wish lists, and almost without a day off, she shops with her list in hand and is known to many of the store managers. They call her up, "Chrissie the clothes you've been looking at are on sale," recruited into the world of orphans. Each Christmas box has the name of its recipient. These aren't generic gift boxes;

these are special and given with as much love as her grandkids get a couple weeks before.

The kids sat on the edge of their seats. For some, this is the first time they will ever hold a Christmas gift in their hands; it's a big deal. One by one they come to the front beaming with the joy of being recognized and the anticipation of what is inside the heavy box now in their hands. Then, the torture begins. They must wait until everyone has their box. Then 10, 9, 8, 7, their hands are on the lid, 6, 5, 4, it's unbearable anticipation, 3, 2, 1! Lids fly across the place— Christmas Day has arrived! To someone who has lived their life in the gray monotony of a cold institution, this is heaven. Sneakers that actually fit, jeans, shirts, tops, sweaters, perfume, makeup. Cheers and laughter fill the place. A year's work exploding in a few seconds. We look on, thankful for these faces we have come to love. They are God's gift to us.

The next day I was sitting in one of the homes at Vatra. The new sofa carried by some of our boys from storage had been put in place in the latest house to be opened. In a few hours, a dozen girls would carry their bags into new bedrooms; they were coming home to Vatra Village. The living room was first to be finished, and I was keeping out of the way as Melody and Chrissie directed each load to the bedrooms upstairs in this stunning new house. I know my lane, and staging a home isn't where my talent lies. Each room had been designed six thousand miles away. Melody knows every corner of the building, she chooses matching colors, duvets, rugs, towels. Each thing fits together, planned a year in advance. I can hardly match socks with shoes, but I can tell the story. I sat on the sofa, proud of the hard work of each part of this miracle. The builders, Nadia, the people who had sacrificed in each service as they heard the story and were moved to help. Ulizana sat on the sofa beside me. I'd hardly noticed I was basking in God's faithfulness. "Dad, the kids have been asking if we can have a church service this Sunday night. I checked already, and we can get the church we used last night."

It was a good idea. All our kids go to church, but to different churches. I'd thought already if I got them together, I could clarify some thoughts I'd had for the future. "Sure, Uli, will you arrange some praise and worship?" Talk about lanes. This girl, whose story I'd told so many times in America, was made for worship. Her eyes lit up, and in a few minutes other kids were coming to me. "Are we having a church service, Dad?" It doesn't take long for news to pass through the "family."

On Sunday night, the chairs were in place, music was arranged, and church was about to happen. The singing was so good. Each house has regular Bible studies, but this felt different. I'd shared in each house many times. This felt so different. There was a cohesion to everything going on. The girls sang, hands raised. The boys were more subdued, but that's the case everywhere. Ulizana introduced me like we were a "real" church. I smiled as I walked to the lectern. I spoke from my heart, the words flowed, we were having real honest church! As I spoke, a thought kept playing over in my head. These kids need a church that understands where they have come from. As I spoke, the thoughts drifted away; this felt so good.

Church was done. I was sitting at the back in a quiet corner. The kids had formed a circle and were singing song after song. The atmosphere was fabulous. I know I'd made ground in their hearts, a priceless gain for the Kingdom. Pavel, one of the house parents approached. "Dad," he looked serious, "we need our own church!" I wasn't the only one thinking during the service.

As soon as Pavel had moved to the side, Catalina, one of the leaders in her house, came and sat on the chair I'd been leaning on in front of me. "Daddy, we need to have our own church!"

Pavel looked over at me and smiled. This was getting serious. Nadia was next. She, too, repeated the sentiments of Pavel and Catalina!

"Okay, Pavel, I want you to look for a building we can rent here in the city." He broke out into an even bigger smile!

Ironically the day before, I'd been telling Chrissie about taking it easy over the next little while. I would concentrate on building the monthly support it would take to support this growing family. New kids would be filling the beds I'd just watched being put in place. Now here I was looking for yet another challenge, starting a new church!

The next morning Pavel texted me, "We have a meeting at 11. About a building." *Already?* I've been in this whirlwind before. God hears a yes and the jigsaw starts falling into place. What happened next still leaves me speechless.

He told me a crazy story. There was a man here in Chisinau that had found the Lord in a prison cell in Germany. He and his brother stole for a living. Caught and jailed, they had finally run out of luck. They had been put in a place where God could meet them. While in jail they grew in faith, and upon their release they returned to Moldova, started a business and had become very successful. This gentleman knew Pavel because he had tried to hire him away from The Orphan's Hands, but Pavel rejected his offer. The businessman even offered several apartments to house the boys that were homeless, in hopes to sweeten the deal. When he realized he was getting nowhere, he then asked Pavel to advise him so he could achieve the same results as we were having with our kids. Their ongoing relationship had brought me to the front seat of Pavel's car as we drove to meet him. The office Pavel took me to was on a street that the brothers had built. They owned most of the tall apartment buildings that lined the road. I recognized the place; it was above the little church where we held our Christmas party. I discovered later he had given the space for the church we'd used a few hours ago.

We were welcomed in. A tall man in his mid-forties rose to meet me, his warm handshake and smile made me feel I was meeting an old friend. Soon I was telling him the events of the last few hours. Then he asked, "How long have you been helping children in orphanages? What is your vision for the kids?" He was now firmly in my lane. I explained how our kids are healed by helping. I told him of the miracle of breaking the orphan spirit in our kids' hearts by urging them to give. Every word was penetrating his mind; his eyes barely blinked, and I knew a connection was being made. Speaking in Russian, Pavel and Nadia took turns translating his response.

"I've been waiting for years to meet someone like you!" It seemed like it was taking ages to get to where he was going. "I have adopted eight orphans; my heart is to care for those in need." I could hardly believe what I was hearing. In Moldova, I have never met anyone with a pure passion for the country. I've heard a lot of remonstrations that ended up in the remonstrator being the recipient of the blessing. This felt different. "Come, I want you to see something," He said as he grabbed his coat, and we went out onto the street and went up around five hundred yards. A four-story building was in front of us. He walked in, climbed a flight of stairs, and opened a door to a huge unfinished space. He turned and fixed my gaze. "I want to give you this building to help you reach my people!" I was in a dream. This entire floor was big enough to hold three or four hundred people. My mind whirred with all the ministry we could undertake in this space. There was enough room to have a coffee shop, office, and recreation center; everything we'd been talking about that is needed to help our kids reach those who have never heard of the redemptive story of Jesus! I stood at the point of tears; this space would be a shortcut to our dreams! Instead of buying land, spending months and years building, we could soon finish the interior and make it the most incredible place to bring a harvest of young lives, brought to the cross by orphans.

This story is still being written; I can't wait for it to unfold. God loves the lost, wherever they may be. He has His people waiting to connect together, some with buildings, some with vision, all for His glory!

Chapter 21
The Bummer Lamb Reward

When I held Andrew in my arms for the first night in that Continental hotel în Timișoara, I had no idea I was holding a lifetime of joy and pain, mountains and valleys, dark nights and sunny days. It has cost me more than I can imagine. It has given me more that I could ever dream. Look around you, God has a phone and there is a bummer lamb out there for you to rescue.

I told you in the story of how I would go with my mother to pick up turnips and how we discovered the little bummer lambs. By being in the presence of the shepherd, held by him and hearing his heartbeat, fed by his hand, warm by his fire and learning to hear his voice... once that little creature was put back out in the field with the other lambs and ship, that lamb knew his shepherd's voice. And while the others were still only thinking about it, the wee lamb was on his way to where he knew he was loved.

Many years ago, we were driving to a church service one day. Andrew was with me and he had been quiet for over an hour. It made me nervous. The seventeen-year-old boy sitting beside me had, I am sure, many questions as to how the events of his life have unfolded. This silence wasn't just an idle silence. There was, I knew, a reason for it. When he finally spoke, "Dad..." then a painful pause. My heart was rapidly beating in my chest. Doubt gripped my stomach. Was he going to say, "I wish you had left me in Romania with my own people?" My mind raced as fast as my heartbeat.

"I've been thinking."

I knew it. He wasn't happy. I glanced over for a second. He had tears in his eyes. I wanted to stop the car, but I was afraid that it would only dramatize even more this moment. "You know, I'd been thinking about becoming a lawyer." My hands squeezed the steering wheel tighter and I tried to normalize my voice. "Yes," I replied. He began again, "Do you think..." and his voice trailed away for a moment. "Do you think that God had me adopted into this family just to be a lawyer?" Now that he had started, his words seemed to give him more courage. "Dad, I want to help you help other kids like me."

Now it was time for tears in my eyes. Here was my bummer lamb, turning his heart towards the vision of my life. He graduated from high school with honors and did the same in college. He stayed home and spent as much time as possible helping in the ministry and for over a decade, if you've seen me, you've seen Andrew. He is driven everyday by the desire to help the bummer lambs who languish in hopelessness, rejected by their own. The pain of his past, the sickness caused by neglect has led my bummer lamb to become a pillar in my life. It's an amazing thing to watch this beautiful young man care so much for the bummer lambs.

So, as you can see, the two major moments of my life started with a phone ringing. When I reached for the phone that cold January morning, I had no idea I was reaching for the handle of a totally new way of life. A third of the century has passed, hundreds of trips across the Atlantic Ocean, millions of dollars and countless lives transformed all because I answered a phone. I learned one thing through this incredible experience: everybody has a phone in their life. If you don't know where yours is, I urge you to find it. It is the mechanism by which God can speak into your life. It is the alarm clock of destiny. It is the tug and pull of the still small voice in the middle of the night. It is the insane thought that is so out of the ordinary that it can't be you, it has to be Him.

I've discovered something else in my life: it is easier to be directed when you're moving than when you're standing still. You may even start off in the diametrically opposed direction, but by moving, His hand can intervene and turn you around without you even realizing it. Many years ago, a TWA flight was hijacked by a terrorist. With a gun to his head, the incredibly brave pilot dared to move the yoke of the airplane... just an imperceptible amount. The small divergence caused the plane to do a complete circle without the terrorists' knowledge, and the pilot landed the plane where it took off.

God has a way of getting you to move. I was merely trying to appease my father for what I thought may be his dying wish after that first phone call. We were established and successful in Romania when the second phone call came. I wasn't interested, I had adopted Andrew from there and that was the world I wanted to transform. If I had barely heard of Romania, I can assure you, I never heard of Moldova. When I crossed the border for the very first time after driving across the Carpathian Mountains a terror filled 3-hour adventure, the first houses I saw were in a village that had been destroyed by an earthquake. Only after many visits and seeing unbearable heartache, did the ruins of that forgotten village come to represent the brokenness of Moldova. I thought Romania was enough. I'd done my bit. I adopted a bummer lamb. I fixed up the place that had been his prison. I had no idea it was a stop off point to where the Guiding Hand was leading me and as you read this, I have no idea where the Hand will lead me to in the future. What I want you to get from reading this testimony is this: make your life count. Do something bigger than the world you live in and your world will become bigger. Comfort is a killer. Risk brings rewards.

Afterthought

The number of girls and boys that we call our own increases almost daily. They complete their education, move on as adults, find their own apartments and jobs, and begin lives with real futures. But they are still our kids, as much as your grown children are yours. I see and hear from them all the time, offer advice, rejoice in their victories.

And meanwhile, there are new orphans coming to our homes all the time. Their stories are tragic, like those who have come before them, but different.

June 1 marks National Children's Day in Moldova. On that fine warm day, there are parties across Moldova celebrating her children, that include music, dancing, balloons, and sweet treats.

For the sixteen-year-olds living in orphanages, it is the beginning of the end. They finish cleaning and painting their rooms. The next day, they are sent away. Not one soul cares what happens to them after that—if they have something to eat, if they have a place to sleep, if they are safe.

No one knows, and no one cares if they are even alive after they leave the orphanage. Who would know?

If you care about this evil called sex trafficking, an industry that is larger than illegal drugs, this is where you must start.

There is no larger pool of vulnerable, easy-to-obtain, fresh-faced girls than the orphans of Moldova. This small nation is the engine for sex trafficking for all of Europe.

Years ago, I had a meeting with the United States ambassador to Moldova, Michael D. Kirby. We sat in his downtown office, and he said, "Philip, the Moldovan girls who are naive enough to get unknowingly into the cars of sex traffickers are beaten, raped, and stripped of their passports within twenty-four hours. They are taken illegally to places like Turkey, Saudi Arabia, and Italy."

These girls are sexually and physically abused over and again by people trained to break the spirit of these girls, until they are ready to do anything for anyone just for the pain to stop. Then they are sold, as often as thirty times a day, to any stranger with a few dollars. If they turn up pregnant, they are beaten again. If they don't miscarry, they are forced to have an abortion. Over and over, they are used, with few living beyond a few years.

I've been discouraged on an occasion, but never doubted what God has called me to do. Together with my Christian friends in the United States, we are building more beds, and more girls and boys will be prevented from being a part of the largest population of slaves history has ever recorded.

You, too, can help us stop sex trafficking in Moldova! With your help, we can provide a safe, loving, Christ-filled home for aged-out orphan girls and boys in Moldova. Next June, another group of innocent kids will be sent away from the state-run orphanages. Help us do more, save more. Help us give them a bright future.

It would take volumes to tell you of all the bummer lambs who have been placed by grace in our care. Many have moved on to make their place in the world, many are now wives, husbands and parents. Each day my social media receives a photo of a little boy or girl who will live a life far removed from the stench and abuse of an orphanage. I'm struck with the determination in so many of these amazing kids' lives to protect their babies from ever becoming "bummer lambs." Sadly, there are still multitudes abandoned, lost, crying in the harvest field waiting for someone to pick them up, wrap loving arms around them, and bring them home.

As I write this, the world has been brought to a standstill by COVID-19 pandemic. The other week I was on the last flight out of Moldova before the entire nation became cut off from the rest of the world. Just before midnight, our flight took off the ground with 20 minutes to spare. On the way to the airport, I gave final instructions to Pavel and Nadia, our main leaders of the ministry in Moldova. I told them that once they dropped us off to go back to Vatra village and shelter in place. I gave them all the reasons I had heard while listening to the news from America.

We got to Istanbul in the wee hours of the morning and found a hotel, as we would be stuck there for four days, and collapsed exhausted in my bed. The next morning, I checked my phone to find pictures of Nadia and Pavel out in the villages feeding families. I texted Nadia, a bummer lamb that was picked up off a bench in the largest orphanage in Moldova.

Years ago, I sat and spoke to Nadia one morning. She barely knew any English and I barely knew any Romanian but through a pantomime and a game of charades, I communicated to her heart that if she was born God, had a plan. I did not realize that day that she heard my heart and her life had been transformed. So, as I rested in my hotel in Istanbul, I sent Nadia a text, "Nadia what are you doing? I told you to stay home." Immediately, the little bubble that alerts you the other person is responding appeared, and in one line she stopped me in my tracks, "Dad I was doing exactly what I knew you would be doing." The proof of a bummer lamb that has heard the shepherd's voice. Everyday Nadia, Pavel, Angela, Vlad, and Jazgul travel across Moldova feeding and loving the broken in the midst of a world that has gone mad over a virus. Nadia is unique but around her are many others who have the same heart.

"The Orphan's Hands" is a literal explanation of what these kids do... the orphan's hands are reaching out to those in need. When I first went to Moldova, I would go to the orphanages and poor homes. But miraculously, as the orphans we rescued became sons and daughters, it quickly became evident that a native-speaking young person who could identify with the orphans and the poor was much more effective than an American that has dropped down from the moon and had no connection to their tragic world. Yet, a redeemed orphan identifies completely with their despair and when they speak of the difference in their life, it rings the bell of hope in the middle of despair.

I hope reading this book short book awakens the Shepherd's heart in yours. We need you in the fields.

Human Trafficking Statistics

Moldova: Tier-2 Watch List

As reported over the past five years, Moldova is primarily a source country for men, women, and children subjected to sex trafficking and forced labor. Moldovan victims are subjected to sex and labor trafficking within Moldova as well as in Russia, the Ukraine, and other countries in Europe, the Middle East, Africa, and East Asia. Women and children are subjected to sex trafficking in Moldova in brothels, saunas, and massage parlors. Increasingly, girls ages thirteen to fifteen are victims of sex trafficking. Child sex tourists, including from the EU, Turkey, Australia, Israel, Thailand, and the United States, subject Moldovan children to commercial sexual exploitation. The breakaway region of Transnistria remains a source for victims of both sex and labor trafficking. Official complicity in trafficking continues to be a significant problem in Moldova.

The highest-ranking source countries for human trafficking—piling up human trafficking statistics daily—include Belarus, the Republic of Moldova, the Russian Federation, the Ukraine, Albania, Bulgaria, Lithuania, Romania, China, Thailand, and Nigeria.

A human trafficker can receive up to 2,000 percent profit from a girl trafficked for sex.

The International Labor Organization estimates that there are 40.3 million victims of human trafficking globally.

- 81% of them are trapped in forced labor.
- 25% of them are children.
- 75% are women and girls.

The International Labor Organization estimates that forced labor and human trafficking is a $150 billion industry worldwide.

The International Labor Organization estimates that there are 4.5 HYPERLINK "http://www.ilo.org/global/about-the-ilo/newsroom/news/WCMS_182109/lang--en/index.htm"_____ HYPERLINK "http://www.ilo.org/global/about-the-ilo/newsroom/news/WCMS_182109/lang--en/index.htm"million HYPERLINK "http://www.ilo.org/global/about-the-ilo/newsroom/news/WCMS_182109/lang--en/index.htm"_____ HYPERLINK "http://www.ilo.org/global/about-the-ilo/newsroom/news/WCMS_182109/lang--en/index.htm"people HYPERLINK "http://www.ilo.org/global/about-the-ilo/newsroom/news/WCMS_182109/lang--en/index.htm"_____ HYPERLINK "http://www.ilo.org/global/about-the-ilo/newsroom/news/WCMS_182109/lang--en/index.htm"trapped HYPERLINK "http://www.ilo.org/global/about-the-ilo/newsroom/news/WCMS_182109/lang--en/index.htm"_____ HYPERLINK "http://www.ilo.org/global/about-the-ilo/newsroom/news/WCMS_182109/lang--en/index.htm"in HYPERLINK "http://www.ilo.org/global/about-the-ilo/newsroom/news/WCMS_182109/lang--en/index.htm"_____ HYPERLINK "http://www.ilo.org/global/about-the-ilo/newsroom/news/WCMS_182109/lang--en/index.htm"forced HYPERLINK "http://www.ilo.org/global/about-the-ilo/newsroom/news/WCMS_182109/lang--en/index.htm"_____ HYPERLINK "http://www.ilo.org/global/about-the-ilo/newsroom/news/WCMS_182109/lang--en/index.htm"sexual HYPERLINK "http://www.ilo.org/global/about-the-ilo/newsroom/news/WCMS_182109/lang--en/index.htm"_____ HYPERLINK "http://www.ilo.org/global/about-the-ilo/newsroom/news/WCMS_182109/lang--en/index.htm"exploitation HYPERLINK "http://www.ilo.org/global/about-the-ilo/newsroom/news/WCMS_182109/lang--en/index.htm"_____ HYPERLINK "http://www.ilo.org/global/about-the-ilo/newsroom/news/WCMS_182109/lang--en/index.htm"globally.

In a 2014 report, the Urban Institute estimated that the underground sex economy ranged from $39.9 million in Denver, Colorado, to $290 million in Atlanta, Georgia.

Every 30 seconds another person becomes a victim of human trafficking.

Appendix

Want to get involved? Here's what you can do:

- Become a monthly partner or give a donation. Visit www.theorphanshands.org/give to give today.

- Join a prayer group. Please pray for us as we pray for you. We invite and encourage you to send in your prayer requests. Each will be prayed over, and your need lifted to the Father by name.

- Start a gift drive. We need new coats, boots, toys, toiletries, and much more. Every year we send a container to Moldova

- Take a mission trip. Change a life while you change your own! Take a group to Moldova, and spend your days ministering to children and teens who have grown up hearing they are worthless.

- Start a fundraising page for The Orphan's Hands. It is simple and will reach people who have never heard of The Orphan's Hands. Join us today, and make your voice even louder for the orphans in our care and for the ones we have yet to reach with the love of Jesus Christ.

- Share our FB page with family and friends. Once you have created an account, add the link to your profile to help tell people about your fundraising.

- Share this book with your friends, family, and especially your Pastor. Invite Philip and The Orphans Hands to share at your church! There are always young ladies here in the USA from Moldova traveling and sharing their amazing story! Their English is nearly perfect; their ministry gifts, beyond measure.
- Contact Andrew Cameron (yes, *that* Andrew) at andrew@theorphanshands.org to schedule Philip and TOH.

Give the orphans a better chance for a better life. By doing any or all of these things, you are changing the lives of every orphan currently in our care and any orphan who comes into our care in the future.

Thank you for reading Our Bummer Lamb! Please share this book with someone so they can know this amazing story!